ATR Publishing

Twelve Teas to Remember

Amy Lawrence

The Cole Family
Happy
Coaching!
Amy Lawrence

Published by:
ATR Publishing

Photos by:
Patrick Lawrence

Back Cover Photo by:
Sirlin Photographers
(916)444-8464
http://www.sirlin.com/

ISBN: 978-0-9855835-2-1

Contents

January

February

March

April

May

June

July

August

September

October

November

December

Dedication and Thank You

I would like to dedicate this book to my husband, Patrick Lawrence. Without him, this book and all of my other books would be nonexistent. Pat has spent countless hours photographing and designing the layout for the book. He is also the man behind my website and online ordering system. He designs my business cards, signs and works the booths at the World Tea Expo, farmer's markets and Northwest Tea Festival. He helps me flavor and pack tea when I'm overwhelmed with orders. He is my best friend, my husband and business partner. Thank you Pat, I love you dearly!

I would also like to thank the following special people:

My boys

Thomas – Thank you for doing all of those dishes when I was creating new recipes and doing the photo layouts for the books. I know it was a massive amount and I really appreciated your help. Also for tasting all of the goodies!

Jacob – For listening to me complain when something wasn't right, for giving me suggestions for names and recipe ideas and for tasting!

My family

Dad – For suggesting that we should do the remodeling work on the new tea shop ourselves and for volunteering to do it. Also for giving me that gorgeous Korean tea pot for the cover of the book.

Mom – For your countless hours of editing and rewording my book. Taking on the wholesale business and opening the tea shop was not part of the plan when I set out to finish this book. You have saved me so many hours of grief with all of your expertise and time.

Joy – For your inspiration and strength.

Stan – For all of your help on the remodeling project and support throughout the years and my "favorite father-in-law".

Michele – For helping me promote the book, helping me in Auburn every year at our annual tea at the Power's Mansion Tea Time, for coming out to help me with the tea shop. You and Stan are both are so supportive of my tea adventures and the best in-laws a person could have. Thank you so much!

My friends

Dena and Chris – Although you didn't help directly on this particular book, some of these recipes you created and helped develop for use in the tea room so many years ago.

Donna – Thank you so much for your inspiration and cheerleading. You've helped me so much! And Spenser, I know you threw ideas out too.

Babette – Thank you for all of the weekly calls, checking to see how far I was, keeping me on track and also for cheerleading as well!

Tina – After our lunch one day, you gave me the final idea that brought the book together. It had been mostly written, waiting on photography but needed something that would tie it all together. Our conversation sparked that idea. Thank you!

Betty – For dusting, arranging and restocking the Antique Trove and for being patient waiting for tea while I was working on this book.

Julie – For your cheerleading, support and the fact that we're always together when I decided to embark on some new tea adventure!

Monique and Amy – For your cheerleading and support!

Last and certainly most important

My customers! – Without you, this would not be book number 11 for me. Many of you have purchased this book without seeing even a picture of it. I really appreciate all of the faith you have in me and I am so grateful for all of your support, especially for all of my California tea room customers who have been with me throughout the years. Thank you!

Introduction

"Your highest purpose isn't solemn or heavy; it's the most playful thing you can do." — Martha Beck

Cooking has been my passion since the 5th grade. At that time my neighbor and a fabulous cook, Ginny Lacy, gave me a Junior Cookbook. Others took an interest in my wanting to cook as well. My grandmother, Alice McCoy, an excellent cook herself, always delighted in showing me new cooking techniques. My mother definitely supported my efforts as she did not share my joy of cooking. She let me have free rein of the kitchen and was happy to do dishes.

Early Induction into Party Planning

From an early age my parents' social life enthralled me. My dad was an officer in the U.S. Army and they attended many parties and balls. Often times my mom was on the various committees that planned the functions and often volunteered my skills to help. I remember many times hand-writing invitations and place cards in calligraphy for a special event (such as the annual Artillery Ball) and I took great pride in creating each one of them. Though I was too young to attend, my mother would return home after the gala event and would describe everything in detail. The elegant foods served especially were intriguing to me.

My love for entertaining really developed during my college years when my father became a battalion commander in Germany. My parents would often have open houses and parties at their house. Sometimes the guest list would include up to one hundred guests. Planning every detail of the menu was pure enjoyment for me (much to my mom's delight). Appetizers and desserts were my favorites to prepare.

At the same time I also enjoyed also the invitations to military functions and parties at a nearby Army post. Though too embarrassed to ask the hostess of one particular New Year's Eve party for the recipe of an appetizer I was taken with, I did muster the courage to inquire about the ingredients. Later I was able to recreate it based on my mental notes. I think it was then I discovered there was no real need for recipes. This opened my mind to create new food dishes based on my palate and cooking experiences.

Despite my love of cooking, I had always wanted to become a special education teacher. I graduated high school, went to college, got my B.S. in Education and continued straight on to get my M.S. in Special Education. I taught learning handicapped students for a few years and eventually moved to California where I taught severely handicapped students – mainly autistic children. Overall I taught for 11 years. I thoroughly enjoyed it but eventually wanted to be home with my two boys. For two years I stayed at home as a full time mom. Though I loved being home I was restless and often thought of pursuing other interests.

The Idea of Opening a Tea Room

During one of my mom's visits from Missouri, we went to tea at the Elegant Garden in Citrus Heights, California (sadly this tea room is now closed). It was there I decided and told my mom, "I want to open a tea room. I love to cook. My experience as an assistant manager of a gift shop in high school and college has given me an appreciation for selling fine gifts and a tea room would encompass both." I think my mom was surprised, but she didn't say much – just supported me as she always does. My dream of opening a tea room became a reality in 2003.

How This Book Came About

I enjoy the planning of a party from the guest list down to the final to-do list. Searching out recipes, finding the perfect favors, decorating the table and, of course, preparing the food are real loves for me. I usually spend considerable time thinking about how everything goes together from the shapes and colors of the sandwiches and desserts to the matching of recipes with the foods in season. If you, perhaps, do not share this love of planning, this book is for you. I have given you to-do lists and forms. For those of you who share my love of planning, I hope you enjoy the details and that this book will inspire you to create your own memorable afternoon tea to remember.

Details are my love! I notice things others do not. My favorite hotel in Monterey, CA, has pineapple lamps. At first glance they don't appear to be pineapples but rather some kind of iron décor. I noticed them right off and commented to my husband, "That's neat! Pineapples are the symbol of hospitality. How clever!" My husband couldn't believe I paid that much attention to detail and told me so.

When I first opened the tea room I quickly discovered the lack of tea sandwich recipes. They all seemed basically the same. I began turning appetizer ideas into tea sandwiches. I searched through old cookbooks for ideas and then added new ingredients to make them my own. Often times when eating out at a restaurant an inspiration for a tea sandwich forms in my mind. I love to experiment with ingredients until I feel the recipe is perfect. My advice to you is to be imaginative when you're planning your menu. You never know what new sandwich or dessert you will create.

So that's how my tea career began. I had no experience other than a love of tea, a love of creating elegant dishes, and love of presenting fine retail merchandise to customers. This background experience along with the passion and the drive to succeed has grown into an online tea merchandising business. Just recently my business also has branched out to the wholesale tea market where I am creating varieties of tea flavorings and blending my own teas.

This book has been in the works for many years, since the tea room days. It has mostly been written for a long time, but since including special pictures was a large part of my vision, I didn't feel we were up to the task quite yet. I had a certain image and idea in my mind, but didn't know quite how we were going to do it. After publishing "Entertaining with Amy", with photos I felt it was finally time for this one. This book is but another chapter in the fulfillment my dreams. Sharing them with you is icing on the cake, so to speak, and I hope you enjoy using it as much as I have enjoyed presenting it to you.

History of Afternoon Tea

There are many books dedicated to the history of afternoon tea. One of my favorites is Jane Pettigrew's, "A Social History of Tea". It has everything you would ever want to know about the history of tea. I highly suggest reading it.

Here are a few quick details about tea:

Catharine of Braganza is credited to bringing the actual tea drinking ritual to England. It is said that when the Portuguese princess arrived to England to marry Charles II in 1662, she brought with her a casket of tea. Because she enjoyed it so much, she made it fashionable in England.

The idea of taking afternoon tea is believed to have been started by the Duchess Anna of Bedford. She had a "sinking feeling", in the middle of the afternoon as there was a long gap between meals. She asked her maid to bring her the necessary equipment to make tea and something small to eat in her private room. She eventually invited others to join her. This idea "taking of tea in the afternoon" developed into a new social event between the late 1830's and early 1840's and thus "afternoon tea" was born.

High tea tends to imply an idea of elegance and sophistication when in reality it was originally an evening meal at around 6 p.m. as laborers returned home. High tea consists of meat and potatoes as well as other foods and tea. It was not exclusively a working class meal but was adopted by all social groups. Families with servants often took high tea on Sundays in order to allow the servants time to go to church.

Various Tea Times

Cream Tea – A simple tea consisting of scones, clotted cream, marmalade or lemon curd and tea time can be whenever you wish.

Low Tea/Afternoon Tea – An afternoon meal including sandwiches, scones, clotted cream, curd, 2-3 sweets and tea. It was known as "low tea" because guests were seated in low armchairs with low side-tables on which to place their cups and saucers.

Royale Tea – A social tea served with champagne at the beginning or sherry at the end.

High Tea – An evening meal enjoyed around 6 p.m. as laborers and miners returned home. This tea consists of meat, potatoes, other dishes and tea.

What Exactly Is Afternoon Tea?

My idea of afternoon tea is getting away for a few hours from your hectic and busy life schedule, sitting down with a good friend or friends and enjoying a fine cup of tea paired with delicious treats. Whether it's just a cup of tea and scones or the entire full afternoon tea – complete with sandwiches and tea desserts, it is relaxing, replenishing and nurturing. The entire experience is like "a spa for your soul".

Whether you visit a traditional tea room or have your own tea party, the experience is the same. Taking tea is about taking time out for yourself and your friends. It is about making connections and building relationships. It is about feeling pampered and special, spending quality time with friends and family. It is not a rushed event. You leisurely sit and talk. You are there to not only eat and drink tea, but even more so to relax and enjoy the moment of friendship.

Planning Your Special Tea

Deciding on the Occasion

One of the first things you need to decide when planning a tea party is, "Why am I having this tea party?" "Is it a special occasion, such as a birthday?" "Do I just want to get together with my friends and have fun?" "Do I want a formal tea with my grandmother's fine china, or do I want a less formal affair and serve just tea and scones?"

Think about how many people you want to invite. Sometimes this alone will determine how detailed you want the tea to be. One thing to remember is that if you are having an afternoon tea with sandwiches, scones and desserts, it will be quite a bit of work. I'm not telling you this to scare you off, but to prepare you for the amount of time it will take to have everything ready. Consider having someone help you, as often people seem to underestimate the time and effort it takes to put on a tea party. One good example of this I relate when I teach a class on having tea parties is about my former cook, Connie. She had been working at the tearoom for a few years. One year she decided to have a tea party at her home for her daughter's birthday and about 8 of her friends. As she was used to cooking for 200 people and more at the tea room she didn't think it would be a big deal. By the time she finished doing everything herself, she was shocked at the amount of work it was. Having help in the tearoom with prepping the sandwiches, garnishing the desserts, and setting the table had not prepared her for doing it alone.

It doesn't matter if you are making sandwiches for 8 or for 200, you still have to make the filling, make all the desserts, and garnish everything. So even though the menu items are small, you still have to go to the work of making them. If you're not into cooking all that food, then get help. It is okay. Buy desserts from the bakery if you're not into baking. Have someone else make a few dishes if you don't have much time to devote to cooking for your party.

You may be like me and want to do it all yourself, if so, just plan ahead. Choose recipes you can make ahead of time and plan it all out so that on the day of your party you're not exhausted. Many desserts can be frozen. Sandwich fillings can be made a few days before and, in fact, often taste better if they are made ahead. Lemon curd and Devonshire cream will keep up to two weeks in the refrigerator. Scones can be made ahead of time and frozen, and just thawed and reheated in foil before the party.

Whatever the occasion, be sure to jot down a few ideas or use this form. This will make planning much easier.

My Afternoon Tea To Remember

Occasion: _____

Theme: _____

Location: _____

Date: _____

Time: _____

Number of guests: _____

Formal: _____   Informal: _____

Invitations: _____ sent _____ R.S.V.P.s received

Menu

Teas which will be served: Black tea _____ (traditional)

Black tea _____ (flavored)

Decaf/Herbal _____ (name)

Green tea _____ (name)

Quiche: _____

Scones: _____

_____

Tea Sandwiches

Name: _____ Type of bread:_____ Open/closed:_____

Name: _____ Type of bread:_____ Open/closed:_____

Name: _____ Type of bread:_____ Open/closed:_____

Tea Desserts

Name: _____ Dish/Cut: _____ Garnish:_____

Name: _____ Dish/Cut: _____ Garnish:_____

Name: _____ Dish/Cut: _____ Garnish:_____

Picking a Theme

You don't have to pick a theme, but it sure is fun! Searching out items for themed parties is a great love for me. I get a big thrill finding just the perfect party favor or decoration that goes along with the theme. You can have a tea party for any occasion or for no specific reason.

My mother has one of the best creative examples I've seen. The first anniversary of her mother's death was approaching. She decided to have a tea party for two friends who had lost their mothers the same year. An angel theme was chosen for the event. She layered the plates with special poems so when one was removed a lovely thought was there to be read. In the middle of the table was a vase of beautiful flowers with little notes on shish kabob sticks. When someone became weepy, the guest was instructed to pull a note out of the vase. Each note had a saying that only mothers would say, such as, "Always wear clean underwear without holes in case you may have to go to the hospital". The idea behind the note was to make the guest laugh. I thought this was such a clever idea and what a way to break up the tension if things became intense.

Afternoon tea party themes could include: a certain color such as a pink themed tea party, a holiday, a special birthday, a friendship, a happiness of any kind, an anniversary of an achievement, a certain movie or specific book. The possibilities are endless! Be creative and above all, have fun with it!

Creating Your Menu

After deciding on the occasion, it is time to decide on your menu. This is the fun part! Creating menus is one of the greatest pleasures for me. Search through old cookbooks, family recipes and magazines. Don't worry if it doesn't specifically say, "tea sandwich". Keep your mind open to new ideas and tastes.

When planning your menu it is important to keep these things in mind:

- **Use Quality Ingredients**

Make the most of that one bite. Tea foods are tiny and every single bite counts.

- **Use Simple Recipes.**

Remember your number of guests – the more guests, the more work. Be mindful of this. Our first Valentine's Day tea at the tea room, we decided to make cute little egg salad sandwiches. We thought it would be great to cut them in heart shapes and then garnish with a smaller heart cut out of bread on top. This sounded like a wonderful idea at the time. Later we realized that meant 3 hearts were needed for each sandwich. This is fine if you have 8 people. 8 people equals 24 hearts, but 100 people equals 300 hearts. See the problem? Keep the number of guests in mind at all times!

- **Use a Different Shape or Look for Each Sandwich and Dessert**

Make some sandwiches open-faced, closed, special cut out, etc. For the desserts, choose a fancy dessert, a bar and a cookie. This provides variety on the tea tray. I like to make what I call one "Whoo hoo!" dessert. It can be a cake or pie which often includes whipped cream or frosting such as Margarita Pie (page 118). Then select a bar cookie such as Chocolate Caramel Bars (page 110) and a tea cookie such as Lemon Blossom Cookies (page 89). Different shapes, colors and tastes all provide an interesting experience.

- **Choose Unique Garnishes for Each One**

Choose an ingredient that's in the recipe for the garnish, such as a rosemary sprig or a pecan half. For the desserts try using whipped cream and sprinkling cinnamon or nutmeg over the top. Instead of frosting the entire dessert, just make a rosette with the frosting and put a chocolate chip (white or dark) into the center of the rosette.

- **Be Mindful About Using the Same Ingredients**

Don't use the same ingredient in everything – especially nuts, garlic, seafood and fruit. Think about your guests' tastes and possible allergies. Unless you know them extremely well, plan your menu around someone not liking a certain ingredient. For example, if you use pecans in the Jamaican Banana Scone, don't use pecans in the other scone. If you are using cinnamon, don't use it in all of your other desserts.

Tips on Making Tea Sandwiches

- **Make your sandwich fillings ahead of time.**

Most fillings can be made at least 3 days ahead.

- **If you are making chicken, always use fresh chicken, not canned.**

- **If you are making a tea sandwich with cream cheese filling always soften the cream cheese before making the filling.**

Add freshly chopped herbs whenever possible. If you add a little sour cream to the cream cheese mixture your fillings will be much easier to spread.

- **Think about color when planning your tea sandwich menu.**

Use a variety of breads – dill rye, dark rye, buttermilk, white, wheat – all work well. Always butter the bread before spreading on the filling, otherwise the filling will "leak" through.

- **Think about your sandwich size and cut.**

If you have a lot of sandwiches to make a cookie cutter is not a good option. Use a serrated knife to cut the sandwich into triangles, squares, or fingers.

- **Make your sandwiches the day before.**

This is one of the best organizing tips I can give you. Lay your slices of bread on a cookie sheet lined with parchment paper. Butter each slice. Add filling. Top with second slice. Place a piece of parchment paper over the sandwiches. Place a damp paper towel over the parchment. Wrap the entire cookie sheet in plastic wrap. Chill overnight. Cut them the day of your event. Use a serrated knife for the best cut. The filling will be cold and solidified so they will slice nicely. If you make them and cut them on the same day it is hard to get a "clean" edge and you'll have more "finger prints", on the sandwiches.

- **Use fresh herbs, or chopped veggies for a sandwich garnish.**

If you're making an olive sandwich, slice an olive and garnish on top. Use a pecan half, if the sandwich has nuts. Try flat parsley or rosemary for a garnish. For a quick garnish, sprinkle a bit of lemon pepper or paprika over the top. For the best sandwich look, always save garnishing for the day of the event.

- **Don't press down when you cut the sandwiches. Otherwise you'll leave dents and fingerprints.**

- **Be careful with parsley garnish so you don't get the "astro turf" look.**

Lightly sprinkle parsley on the sides, don't dip.

- **Be careful of spreads that have liquid.**

Too much liquid makes them hard to cut nicely.

- **Try to handle sandwiches as little as possible.**

- **Work with your filling so that you have the correct amount.**

If you have too little filling, the sandwich will taste only of bread.

- **Keeping the sandwiches moist**

After you arrange your sandwiches and flower decorations on the tea tray, cover with a damp paper towel and refrigerate until serving time. This prevents the sandwiches from drying out. Remove the paper towel only moments before the guests begin to eat.

How To Make Your Tea Party More Intimate

When planning your table, think about the guests and the place settings. How can you make it personalized just for them?

Ideas for Special Touches

- **Make personalized name cards for each guest.**

One way to make your party more intimate is by using place cards. People love being recognized and seeing their name at the table. It says, "You thought of me!" They can be as simple as a folded card with their handwritten name or a special place card holder with the name written in calligraphy. I've even used small photo frames with the name written on a piece of paper under the glass. During the holidays you can find cute shaped frames such as stockings or snowmen frames.

- **Try creative napkin folds**

Folding napkins creatively at each place setting always adds a unique touch. There are napkin books with intricate folds, creative examples and how-tos on the internet or just design a simple one yourself. Try using napkin rings or fresh flowers or herbs tied around the napkin for a special effect. Rosemary works very well tied as a napkin ring.

- **Use fresh flowers.**

In addition to using them on napkin rings, fresh flowers always make the table come alive. Try tucking flowers into a tea pot or a tea cup for a centerpiece. If you are having a small tea party, consider tiny bud vases in front of each place setting or tuck a flower in the folds of a napkin.

- **Use decorated sugar**

Mix white sugar cubes with a few decorated cubes.

- **Have guests bring and wear hats.**

When some people are first invited to a tea, they may feel a bit apprehensive. This is normal. Some may think it might be an "uppity" affair and may feel self conscious about what they are wearing or about dining etiquette. Wearing hats breaks the stiffness and relaxes the guests.

- **Garnish your tea tray for a gorgeous effect.**

Try using leaves from your garden such as scented geraniums, mint, oregano, basil and savory. If the plants are not edible and are for decoration only, inform the guests. I like to use geranium leaves underneath the sandwiches and tuck baby's breath and carnations around the tray.

- **Offer guests several different types of tea.**

Be sure to include a tisane (herbal) or decaffeinated tea.

- **Use tea cozies or tea warmers to keep the tea warm.**

More Special Touches

- **Chairs wrapped with ribbons gives them a festive look.**
- **Layered plates add texture to your table.**
- **Special notes or quotes are always appreciated.**
- **Spray painting leaves gives a dynamic effect.**

- **Use fine china and old lace tablecloth linens.**

Don't worry about it all matching. On place settings, alternate 2 different sets of dishes. This brings the look all together yet all the dishes do not have to match. Or make each place setting different.

- **Give your guests a memento of your special event as you say goodbye.**

Cute little tea pot ornaments, decorated frames, or even a box of decorated sugar will make that lasting impression as they walk out the door. Tiny picture frames are nice parting gifts as well. Later you might give them a photo taken of them at your tea to put in it.

Choosing the Right Teas

When choosing teas for your special day, always choose at least 3-4 different kinds. Unless you know your guests' specific tea tastes, I suggest a traditional black tea, a flavored black tea, a decaffeinated tea and an herbal tea.

Assam, Ceylon, Yunnan, Darjeeling and English Breakfast are great choices for the traditional black teas. Flavored teas are also quite popular. From experience with my customers, I would highly recommend a flavored black tea. French Caramel Crème Brule was always the favorite at the tea room, followed by a fruity tea called Southern Hospitalitea. Decaffeinated tea and herbal teas are particularly important for baby showers as many of the guests themselves tend to be pregnant and are conscious about their caffeine intake.

Tea Equipment

One of my good tea friends, James Norwood Pratt, is very emphatic about distinguishing the terms brewing and steeping. He proclaims, "Coffee is brewed, tea is steeped."

Essential Equipment / Tea Accoutrements

- **Kettle or glass container**

When making tea you really only need a few essential pieces of equipment. You need something in which to boil the water. This can be the traditional tea kettle or electric kettle or you can even use a glass container and heat the water in the microwave. The tea kettle is best, but if you are in an office setting, the microwave will do.

- **Infuser**

You will need a tea infuser of some kind. A tea ball, a pincher type mesh strainer, paper filter, or a stainless steel infuser basket will all work for a cup of tea and depending on the size may work for a pot of tea. There are also individual strainers to pour your tea through to your cup as you drink. Personally those are not my favorite as it is quite a bit of work just to drink one cup of tea and often can be messy. The tea sock (cotton infuser) and tea pocket (make your own tea bag) are also infusers and work well for both a cup of tea as well as a pot of tea. Decanting or removing the tea leaves is a matter of preference. Although the English often leave their leaves in the tea pot, I prefer to decant my entire pot of tea before it arrives to the table. If you leave the infuser and leaves in the tea pot, by the time you finish your tea may become bitter.

- **Tea cup or pot**

You need something in which to brew the tea. This may be a cup, mug, or tea pot.

Additional Helpful Equipment

- **Measuring spoon**

Loose tea can be measured with a teaspoon or tablespoon. You can also buy tea measuring spoons such as "the Perfect Cup or Pot of Tea Spoon", for this specific purpose. Some of us however, do not need a spoon and when you feel experienced you can even "pinch" out the right amount of tea with your fingers.

- **Tea cozy or tea warmer**

For me a tea cozy is essential as I do not like to drink cold tea. It is amazing how fast the tea cools without something around the pot or a tea light underneath.

- **Sugar tongs**

- **Sugar bowl**

- **Small milk pitcher**

- **Teaspoons**

for stirring tea

Not Needed But Fun Accoutrements and Added Touches

There are so many unique accessories you can use. The list is endless and full of possibilities. These are a few of my favorites:

- **Drip catchers**

These can be paper doilies or and the hook, sponge and elastic type which go on the end of your tea pot spout. They help stop the drips from running down the side of the tea pot. Some tea pots drip more than others and can make a mess of your tablecloth.

- **Lemon squeezer**

This is for adding lemon to your tea. Place a wedge of lemon inside and squeeze. They come in a variety of forms. My favorite is the lemon bird.

- **Lace Doilies**

Place a lace doily over the milk pitcher for an extra special touch. You can even decorate the lace with beads to help weigh down the cover.

- **Decorated sugars**

You can make them in all colors and shapes. They add a special touch to your party. I love to coordinate them with the season such as roses and hearts for Valentine's Day, shamrocks for a St. Patrick's Day tea and berries and holly for the holiday season. Add a few of the fancy ones on top of the regular white sugar cubes in the sugar bowl for a nice effect. Doing this enables you to conserve them while creating a dramatic contrast with the white sugar cubes.

Molded Sugar

Put 4½ cups sugar in a medium mixing bowl.

In a small glass, measure 3 T. water.

Dip toothpick into coloring and then dip into measured water.

Stir until paste is dissolved.

Pour colored water into sugar.

Mix well with hands making sure all the color is evenly distributed throughout the sugar.

Pack sugar mixture into mold as firmly as possible. Press down on each figure. Using a knife scrape off excess sugar back into bowl. Keep bowl covered with a wet towel as mixture dries out very quickly.

Very Carefully Follow These Steps to Finish Your Sugars

Place a piece of parchment paper over mold.

Place a thin sheet of cardboard on top of parchment.

Carefully flip mold over onto a table top or cookie sheet.

Slide out cardboard.

Carefully without moving the mold, tap each figure until it releases.

Let sugar dry overnight. Store in a cool and dry place.

Ingredients

- 4½ cups super-fine sugar
- 3 T. water
- icing coloring – concentrated paste – we use Wilton
- clear plastic molds – try to choose molds that are small and produce bite-sized sugars.

19

Temperature Guidelines

- Black – 190°-202°
- Oolong – 180°-190°
- Green – 160°-180°
- White – 150°-160°
- Herbal – 212°

Times

- Black 3-5 minutes
- Oolong 3-4 minutes
- Green 1-3 minutes
- White 1-5 minutes
- Herbal 5-7 minutes

Steeping the Perfect Pot of Tea

Fill the tea kettle with freshly drawn water.

Bring kettle to the proper temperature for the tea you are using.

Add one teaspoon of tea per cup to your infuser and put into cup or pot.

Pour water over the leaves.

Replace lid or cover cup.

Steep for proper amount of time for the tea you are using.

Remove infuser.

Stir and serve.

This is just a guideline for steeping tea. Feel free to experiment. Some people may prefer heaping teaspoons, while others prefer less tea. Oolongs can be resteeped and are often taste better the second or third infusion.

As far as temperature goes, the lighter the tea, usually the cooler the water. Be careful not to steep green tea in boiling water. It cooks the leaves and makes the tea bitter.

Equipment and Tips for Serving Large Parties

- **Electric Coffee Urn**

For large parties, an electric stainless steel coffee urn works well. Large coffee maker urns hold about 40 cups. Make sure the urn has not been previously used for coffee as it will affect the taste of the tea. Take out the percolator filter. Place water in the urn, turn it on and wait until the water is heated. Then place your cup or pot under the urn and dispense hot water over your infuser in the cup or pot. The water is not quite as hot as a kettle but it will definitely work for large parties.

You can either make the tea ahead of time in them, or just use the water from them and make individual pots.

- **Air Pots**

These typically hold 2½ pots (6 cup pots) of tea. Warm the air pot first by filling it with warm water (not hot). If you use hot water directly into a cold air pot, the lining will break because they are often made of glass. I like to fill the airpots with warm water and allow them to sit overnight before I fill them with tea the next morning.

- **Tea Cups**

Use different cups if you don't have enough of the same pattern. For extremely large parties, ask various people to be in charge of each table and have them bring a set of six cups for their table.

- **Helpful Tea Measurements**

250 cups equals approximately 1 lb. of tea.

Tips for Making Your Tea Party Stress-Free

- **Plan ahead so you can really enjoy the day of your party.**

- **Ask for help.**

Don't be afraid to ask others to help you serve, make tea, or clean up.

- **Make up a time schedule so you know when to make each item.**

Fillings taste better when made a few days before. Scones can be made ahead of time, frozen and reheated the day of the party.

- **Set your table the night before or even a few days before the party.**

Spend time making it exactly as you want it. If it is an outdoor party, plan an alternative location in the house, just in case it's too warm outside, rainy or buggy.

- **Plan your tea party around your best time.**

If you're an early morning person, then 11 a.m. is fine. If you are a late riser then consider a late afternoon tea. Give yourself plenty of time to be ready.

How to Host a Successful Children's Tea Party

When planning a tea party for children, it doesn't have to be a big affair. Just tea and dessert is often enough. Here are a few tips to hosting a great party.

- **Keep the guest list short**

Invite 3-6 children. It's nice if they all fit around the table, otherwise it can become a zoo.

- **Keep the time short**

1 hour works great, 2 hours maximum.

- **Serve kid friendly foods**

Peanut butter sandwiches, cinnamon toast sticks, and cream cheese with cinnamon and sugar sandwiches are great choices.

- **Use interesting shapes**

Cut the peanut butter sandwiches using fun-shaped cookie cutters.

- **Use real china**

It makes them feel grown-up. Many will want to act more mature when given the chance.

- **Serve them tea**

Sugar Plum Fairy Decaf is a great one for kids. You can add sugar and add a few ice cubes. If they don't want tea you may want to serve milk in their cups.

- **Send out special party invitations**

Handmade invitations make the party even more special. You can cut out tea pot shaped invitations by tracing a tea pot cookie cutter. Your own children will probably be eager to assist in the making of them for additional fun.

- **To save your chairs, dress them in white sheets tied with colored ribbons.**

- **Make sure you have a cute party favor at the end.**

A child's tea cup, colored sugar, a tiny spoon or a small book would work fine.

- **Use name cards.**

Children love to see their name on the table.

- **Try doing a dessert tea if you don't want to make sandwiches.**

- **On the day of the event, be sure to set expectations.**

"This is a special tea party. Everyone is all dressed up. We are using real grown-up china and having a real tea party. So today I want everyone to use their best manners." Ask them, "What are some good manners? Does anyone know?"

- **Above all, relax and have fun!**

12 Teas to Remember

In the following pages, are menus and recipes for the months of the year. Some are light teas, some are full afternoon teas and there's even a savory cream tea. You don't have to make everything on the menu. If you don't want to make the soup, then leave it out. If you feel you want to add another sandwich to the menu, go right ahead. Or if you feel one dessert is enough, then just make one. These are merely suggestions. Typically at our tea room we served 3 menus: cream tea, light afternoon tea and full tea.

- **Cream tea**

This tea is one of the easiest teas to host. All you have to do is make a batch of scones and heat some water for the tea. You can make or buy your lemon curd/Devonshire cream or just serve some good jelly or preserves to go with them. Nothing is finer than a hot scone, hot cup of tea and some great company.

- **Light afternoon tea**

This tea can include so many different menu items. You may include 1-2 freshly made scones, 3 delicious tea sandwiches and 3 decadent desserts for each guest.

- **Full afternoon tea**

At our tea room full afternoon tea included: a slice of Black Forest Ham Quiche, a cup of soup or salad depending on the season, 2 scones, 3 tea sandwiches and 3 tea desserts.

Having a tea party is all about the details – the cute little sandwiches, the elegant tableware, the decorated sugar, etc. When you are having a tea for your friends you want them to feel special and pampered. This is not the get-together barbeque of hamburgers and hotdogs. You want to make that perfect impression when your guests walk through your door as well as that lasting impression as you wave goodbye. Spend some time thinking how to make it a memorable experience for them. With a little planning, and by adding a few special detailed touches, you can create a tea party they will remember fondly.

I hope this book inspires you to create your own memorable tea parties. Happy planning and tea partying!

January

Winter White Afternoon Tea

∾ Soup

Italian White Bean Soup

∾ Scones

Smoked Cheddar and Pear Scones

∾ Tea Sandwiches

Smoked Almond Chicken
Roasted Garlic and Herb Cucumber

∾ Tea Desserts

Toasted Coconut Tea Cakes
Cinnamon Oodle Bundles
Pear Pie

∾ Tea Suggestions

White Ginger Orange Peach
Keemun
Crème Brule Chocolate Chai with milk and sugar

Italian White Bean Soup

- 3 (14 oz.) cans white beans
- 2 (14 oz.) cans diced tomatoes
- 1 T. Italian seasoning
- salt and pepper to taste
- ¼ c onion, chopped
- 3 cloves garlic, minced
- 1 T. olive oil
- Parmesan cheese for garnish

Sauté onion and garlic in olive oil. Add 1 can of white beans. Use an immersion blender to emulsify beans until they have the consistency of "refried beans", or smash with a fork.

Add the remaining beans and the tomatoes. Mix in the Italian seasoning. Add salt and pepper to taste. Heat thoroughly. Serve in glass tea t or small bowls and garnish with parmesan cheese.

Makes about 8 servings (½ c. each)

Smoked Cheddar and Pear Scones

- 3 c. self-rising flour
- ⅛ c. sugar
- ½ c. - ¾ c. white cheddar cheese, shredded (living in Seattle, I like Beecher's "Flag Ship" cheese)
- 2 ripe pears or 1 can of pears drained
- 1 stick unsalted butter
- 1 c. buttermilk (sometimes you may need to add a bit more)
- 2 T. Lapsang Souchong tea

Preheat oven to 400°. Prepare Lapsang Souchong tea by bringing 1 c. water almost to a boil. Add 2 T. Lapsang Souchong tea. Steep for 5 minutes. Strain. Slice pears and submerge them into the tea. Allow to sit for about 5-10 minutes.

Combine self-rising flour and sugar. Cut in butter until mixture is course and crumbly. Add cheese. Drain pears, reserve tea. Add pears and ¼ c. of the Lapsang Souchong tea to the flour mix. Add just enough buttermilk to make a soft dough. Scoop out about ⅓ of the dough and form a small disc about ½ inch thick. Cut into 8 pie-shaped pieces. Do this for the remaining dough. Place on a cookie sheet lined with parchment paper and bake until done, about 8-12 minutes. Makes about 24 scones.

Smoked Almond Chicken Tea Sandwiches

Mix together first 4 ingredients. Add just enough mayonnaise to bind the mixture together. Spread butter on bread. Add filling and top with second slice. Cut into desired shapes about 4 tea sandwiches per sandwich. Sprinkle sliced almonds and parsley on sides of sandwiches for decoration if desired.

Makes about 16 tea sandwiches.

- 2 c. cooked chicken – pulse in food processor or chop finely
- 3 T. green onions, sliced thinly
- ¼ c. smoked almonds – chopped
- salt to taste
- mayonnaise
- butter
- bread
- sliced almonds for decoration – if desired
- parsley for decoration – if desired

Ingredients

- 8 cloves garlic
- 2 T. fresh basil, chopped
- ½ t. dried thyme
- 2 T. fresh chives, chopped
- ⅔ c. cream cheese – softened
- ¼ c. mayonnaise or sour cream
- ⅛ t. salt
- pepper
- butter
- bread rounds (use any kind of bread you would like, I especially like to use dill bread or buttermilk bread, cut the bread into round circles, or interesting shapes. You can also cut the bread ahead and store in the freezer.)

Roasted Garlic and Herb Cucumber Tea Sandwiches

Wrap garlic cloves in foil. Bake at 500° for 30 minutes. Squeeze cloves to extract garlic pulp. Discard skins.

With food processor on, drop garlic, basil, and thyme through food chute; process until minced. Add cream cheese and remaining ingredients; process until smooth.

Butter bread slices, spoon a small amount of the roasted garlic mixture on a bread slice. Top with a cucumber slice. Sprinkle with a little black pepper.

Makes about 1 c. of spread or about 32 tea sandwiches.

Toasted Coconut Tea Cakes

Cakes

Preheat oven to 375°. Mix cake mix, pudding, oil, rum, water and vanilla/coconut extract together in a large mixing bowl. Gradually add eggs one at a time and mix 3 minutes on medium speed until well blended. Bake for 8-15 minutes until golden brown or when done when a toothpick is inserted. Cool for a few minutes and then invert on wire rack and cool completely. You may need to run a small knife around the edge of the cakes before inverting pan.

Glaze

Mix all glaze ingredients together. Dip cooled cakes into glaze and top with toasted coconut. Makes about 40 mini bundt cakes. (Each bundt pan has 12 cakes on a pan.)

Toasted Coconut

Spread coconut on a cookie sheet. Toast at 375° for 5-6 minutes until lightly brown.

Ingredients

Cakes

- 1 box yellow golden cake mix
- 1 lg. box "toasted coconut" instant pudding or "coconut cream" instant pudding
- 4 eggs
- ½ c. vegetable oil
- ¾ c. rum
- 1¼ c. water
- 1 t. vanilla or coconut extract

Glaze

- 4 oz. cream cheese softened
- ¼ c. canned coconut milk or whipping cream
- 1 box powdered sugar
- 1 t. coconut extract
- toasted coconut for garnish (see directions)

Ingredients

- 1½ c. flour
- 1½ c. oatmeal (not instant)
- 2 t. cream of tartar
- 1 t. baking soda
- ¼ t. salt
- 1 T. cinnamon
- ½ c. (1 stick) of unsalted butter
- ½ c. butter-flavored Crisco
- ¾ c. sugar
- ¾ c. brown sugar
- 2 eggs
- 1 t. vanilla
- extra cinnamon and sugar to for rolling cookie balls

Cinnamon Oodle Bundles

Preheat oven to 400°. Line baking sheets with parchment paper.

Grind oatmeal in the food processor until fine.

In a medium bowl, mix together flour, ground oatmeal, cream of tartar, baking soda, salt and cinnamon. Set aside.

Cream sugars, shortening and unsalted butter until light and fluffy (about 2 minutes) with mixer. Scrape sides of bowl often. Add eggs and vanilla. Beat well. Add dry ingredients.

In a small bowl, combine sugar about ¼ c. and 1-2 T. cinnamon. Use a small ice-cream scoop to form balls of dough. I like to use one that is 1½ inches in diameter or you can use the "cup" size of the perfect tea pot spoon. Spray with cooking spray before scooping the first cookie. Hit against side of bowl. Roll balls in cinnamon/sugar mixture and place on prepared baking pans about 2 inches apart. Bake about 6-8 minutes. After removing cookies from oven, leave on pans for about 5 minutes before removing them to wire racks. Store in an airtight container. If you add a slice of bread to the container, the cookies will stay soft. If you use the small 1½ inch scoop this recipe will make about 92 small tea cookies.

After completely cooled, stack in 3's or 4's and tie with a ribbon.

Pear Pie

Preheat oven to 350°. Combine sugar, egg, flour, vanilla and salt. Mix. Fold in sour cream and pears. Pour into shell. Bake for 15 minutes. Remove.

Sprinkle crumb mix on top, return to oven and bake 30 minutes more or until brown. Scoop and place into small glass dishes. Top with whipped cream and sprinkle cinnamon over the top.

Ingredients

- 3 c. cubed pears
- ½ c. sugar
- 1 beaten egg
- 1 c. sour cream
- 1 T. flour
- 1 t. vanilla
- ½ t. salt
- 1 unbaked pie shell

Crumb mix topping

- ⅔ c. flour
- ⅓ c. brown sugar
- ¼ c. butter

February

Valentine's Day Afternoon Tea

❧ Soup

Tomato Basil Bisque

❧ Scone

Coconut Lace Scones with Raspberry Lemon
Curd and Devonshire Cream

❧ Tea Sandwiches

Heart Shaped Chicken Puff Pastry
Tomato Cucumber Kabobs
Strawberry Heart

❧ Tea Desserts

Raspberry Lemon Tartlets
Decadent Chocolate Pearl Cakes
Cherry Shortbread Cookies

❧ Tea Suggestions

Chocolate Raspberry Truffle Tea
Winter Raspberry Champagne Iced served in Champagne Flutes

Ingredients

- ½ c. onion, finely chopped
- ¼ c. flour
- 4 c. tomatoes, finely chopped/puréed
- 1 t. dill seed
- 1 t. dill weed
- 1 t. oregano
- 3 c. chicken stock
- ¼ c. honey
- 1 c. cream
- ¼ c. chopped parsley
- ¼ c. chopped basil
- 4 T. butter

Tomato Basil Bisque

Sauté onions in butter. Add flour, tomatoes, and spices. Add chicken stock and bring to a boil.

Simmer for 15 minutes. Add honey, cream, parsley, and basil. Heat thoroughly.

Add salt and pepper to taste. Makes about 16 (½ c.) servings.

Enjoy!

Coconut Lace Scones with Raspberry Lemon Curd

Preheat oven to 400°. Combine self-rising flour and sugar. Cut in butter until mixture is coarse and crumbly. Mix in coconut and chips. Add just enough of buttermilk mixture to make a soft dough. Scoop out about ⅓ of the dough and form a small disc about ½ inch thick. Cut into 8 pie-shaped pieces. Do this for the remaining dough. Or you can cut scones into shapes with simple shaped cookie cutters. Place on a cookie sheet lined with parchment paper and bake until done, about 8-12 minutes Makes about 24 scones.

Scones are served best warm and may be reheated in foil before serving.

See recipe for Raspberry Lemon Curd on page 44.

Ingredients

- 3 c. self-rising flour
- ½ c. sugar
- ½ c. white chocolate chips
- 1 stick unsalted butter
- 1 c. buttermilk
- ½ c. coconut

Ingredients

- ½ c. butter
- 1 c. granulated sugar
- ½ c. lemon or lime juice
- 3 eggs

Lemon/Lime/Raspberry Curd

This recipe is very versatile. You can use lemon or lime juice to make lemon or lime curd.

Melt butter in microwave for 1 minute. Beat eggs in a glass bowl with an electric mixer until frothy. Mix in butter, sugar, juice and zest. Microwave on HIGH for 3 minutes.

Beat mixture again until smooth. Microwave on HIGH for another 3 minutes. Beat mixture again until smooth. Refrigerate until set/cool.

Makes about 1 cup of curd. Curd will keep up to 2 weeks in refrigerator.

To make raspberry lemon curd, make lemon curd first and then stir in about 3 T. puréed raspberries.

Ingredients

- 1 8 oz. pkg. cream cheese, softened
- 2 c. powdered sugar
- ½ freshly squeezed lemon
- 2 t. vanilla
- 1 c. sour cream

Devonshire Cream

This is not a "true" Devonshire cream, but our customers love our version.

In a small bowl with an electric mixer, beat cream cheese, lemon juice, and vanilla. Gradually beat in powdered sugar. Fold in sour cream.

Makes 1½ cups.

Heart Shaped Chicken Puff Pastry

Thaw pastry sheets about 20-30 minutes. Do not thaw longer or they will be too sticky to use.

While pastry is thawing, cut chicken breasts into tiny pieces. Place oil in skillet, add chicken, garlic and other ingredients on the list that sound appealing to you (except cheeese and cream cheese). Sauté until chicken is done. Cool slightly.

Cut puff pastry into squares or heart shapes. Place on a cookie sheet lined with parchment paper. Add filling, sprinkle with cheese if desired and dot with a cube of cream cheese. Fold over and seal with fingers or fork. For hearts, add a second heart on top and crimp with a fork. At this point you can freeze them if you wish. If you plan on freezing them, freeze directly on cookie sheet first for at least 15 minutes. Then transfer to ziplock freezer bags.

When ready to bake, place on a cookie sheet lined with parchment paper. Thaw for about 15 minutes. Brush with beaten egg.

Bake at 400° until golden (about 10-20 min depending on size).

Ingredients

- 1 package puff pastry
- 2 chicken breasts
- ½ onion, chopped
- 1 T. olive oil
- 1 garlic clove
- cheese – any kind, I like to use smoked cheddar
- tarragon, fresh, chopped
- mushrooms, chopped
- rosemary, fresh, chopped
- bacon, cooked and finely crumbled
- asparagus, cut into very small pieces, microwave for 1 minute, cool
- green onion, finely chopped
- ham, finely chopped
- cream cheese, cut into dice sized cubes
- beaten egg

Ingredients

- small cherry tomatoes
- mozarella pearls or mozarella slices cut into cubes
- cucumber, cut into slices and quartered
- fresh basil
- freshly cracked pepper
- balsamic vinegar – use a good quality one.
- cocktail toothpicks, the longer the better

Tomato Cucumber Kabobs

Throughly wash tomatoes, cucumber and basil. Pat dry. Skewer tomato, cucumber, mozarella and basil leaf.

Serve with balsamic vinegar or Italian dressing if desired.

Strawberry Heart Tea Sandwiches

See recipe on page 84.

Raspberry Lemon Tartlets

I just love this recipe. It's based on my lemon curd recipe and is so easy, yet looks elegant. I prefer the Pepperidge Farm Mini Tart Shells, but I can't always find them. They are in the freezer section. If I can't find them I use the phyllo cups as they work very well too.

Melt butter in microwave for about 1 minute. Beat eggs in a glass bowl with an electric mixer until frothy. Mix in butter, sugar, and lemon or lime juice. Microwave on high for 3 minutes. Beat mixture again until smooth. Microwave again for another 3 minutes. Beat mixture again until smooth. Refrigerate until set. Lemon or lime curd will keep up to 2 weeks in refrigerator.

To make tarts

Fill tart or phyllo cup with about 1 t. of lime curd. Top with an upside down raspberry and sprinkle lime zest over the top. Serve immediately or place in the refrigerator until ready to serve.

Makes about 30 tarts.

Ingredients

- ½ c. butter
- 1 c. sugar
- ½ c. lemon or lime juice
- 3 eggs
- 2 pkg. mini tarts or phyllo cups
- fresh raspberries, rinsed and drained
- zest of 2 lemons or limes

Ingredients

Cake

- 1 box Pillsbury Devil's Food cake mix
- ½ c. unsalted butter, softened
- 3 eggs
- 1¼ c. buttermilk
- 1 t. vanilla
- 3 T. rum (optional)

Chocolate Buttercream Frosting

- 2 c. unsalted butter, softened
- 2 T. rum
- 1 t. vanilla
- 5½ c. powdered sugar
- 2 c. semisweet chocolate chips, melt in microwave and slightly cooled
- 3-5 T. milk

Decadent Chocolate Pearl Cakes

I love making cakes from scratch. However sometimes when you are putting on a tea, it's nice to have a quicker and easier dessert. I doctored this cake mix up a bit and added a very decadent homemade frosting. The pearls add the final elegant touch. You can find them at many kitchen and party supply stores.

Cake

Preheat oven to 350° In a large mixing bowl, add cake mix, eggs, butter, buttermilk, vanilla and rum. Mix on low speed until combined. Scrape down sides of the bowl. Mix on medium speed for 2 minutes. Distribute batter evenly among cupcake liners. Bake about 18-25 minutes until done. Makes 24 cupcakes. These would also be great with the mini cupcake pans.

Chocolate Buttercream Frosting

Cream butter in mixer at high speed for about 2-3 minutes. Gradually add powdered sugar. Stir in rum and vanilla. Stir in melted chocolate and mix until well blended. Add enough milk to desired consistency. Frost cooled cupcakes. After you frost your cupcakes, dip a knife into a cup of milk and lightly spread over the already frosted cupcakes. This smoothes out the frosting. Place in refrigerator until set. Keep in a cool place until ready to eat.

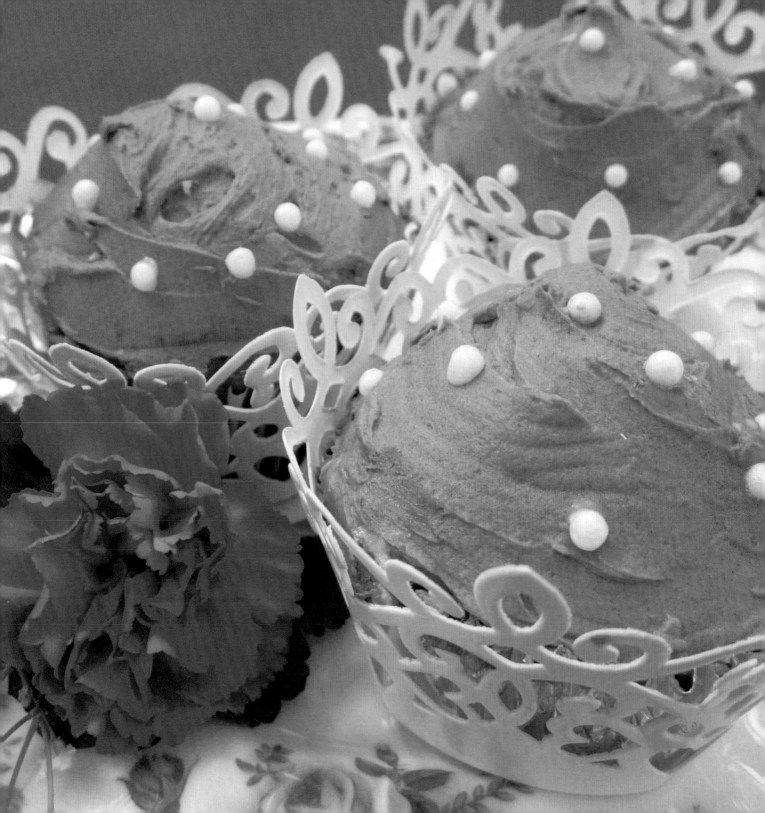

Cookie

- 1 c. butter
- ½ c. sugar
- 1 t. vanilla
- 2 c. flour
- ½ c. white chocolate chips
- ¾ c. dried cherries, cut into tiny pieces

White Chocolate Glaze

- 1 c. white chocolate chips
- 2 t. oil

Cherry Shortbread Cookies

Preheat oven to 350°.

Cream together in a large mixer butter, sugar, and vanilla. Add flour and mix well. Stir in 1 c. white chocolate chips and dried cherries. Scoop with an icecream scoop into balls (use about a 1½ inch). Flatten each ball slightly. Place on a baking sheet lined with parchment paper about 1 inch apart. Bake for 8-12 minutes or until lightly browned. Cool completely before dipping in glaze.

To make glaze, melt 1 c. white chocolate chips in the microwave until melted. Add 2 t. oil and stir well.

Dip half of each cookie into melted chocolate. Allow to dry before serving. Makes about 40 cookies.

There are 2 different looks to this cookie.

Mound Look

After you scoop them out, put them on a cookie sheet and freeze them for about 5 minutes Then bake.

Flat Cookie

Bake them right away after making them.

These freeze very well. Just ball up dough, place on cookie sheet and flash freeze for 10 minutes. Then transfer to ziplock bags or airtight freezer container. When ready to bake, thaw completely for the "flat" look, or thaw partially for the "mound" look.

Cookie Tips and How To Dress up a Cookie

Tips on Making Cookies

Before making cookie dough, it's best to let your butter sit out for a while and soften. It won't hurt butter to sit out overnight. After making your dough, scoop out into cookies using an ice cream scoop. For the cookies in this book, I have used a small 1½ inch in diameter ice cream scoop. You can find this size at most restaurant supply stores. It's usually the smallest one they have. This size makes tiny cookies, perfect for afternoon teas.

After you scoop out your dough, place it on parchment paper lined cookie sheets. If the dough has been out a while and it's soft, then put the cookies in the freezer for about 2 minutes. If the butter is too soft, the cookies will spread everywhere when you bake them. Putting them in the freezer for a bit makes them come out nicely. Consequently if the cookies are frozen, then let them thaw about 10 minutes before baking, otherwise they won't spread at all and will be cookie mounds. Cookie mounds are also another cute look so if you want that look, then bake them slightly frozen.

Dress up a Cookie

You can dip half of it in white or dark chocolate.

Take a small amount of chocolate chips. Put in a small bowl. Microwave for about 20 seconds. Stir then microwave until completely melted. If the consistency is too thick, add a few drops of vegetable/canola/olive oil and stir.

Dip cookie, place on parchment and allow to dry completely.

Drizzle Chocolate

Do the same as above, but use a bit more oil to thin out the chocolate. Take a spoon and lightly go back and forth over the cookie with the chocolate. Allow to dry completely.

March

St. Patrick's Day Afternoon Tea

✌ Soup

Cream of Spinach Soup

✌ Scones

Jamaican Banana Scones with Lime Curd

✌ Tea Sandwiches

Rosemary Chicken
Corned Beef
Cucumber Striped Flowers

✌ Tea Desserts

Pistachio Pudding with Raspberry Jam
Mandarin Orange Cake
Sea Salt Toffee

✌ Tea Suggestions

Irish Breakfast
Irish Creme
Bourbon Slush

Jamaican Banana Scones

Preheat oven to 400°. Combine self-rising flour and sugar. Cut in butter until mixture is coarse and crumbly. Mix in mashed bananas. Add ¾ cup of buttermilk and stir. If mixture is too dry add a little more buttermilk. Add just enough of buttermilk mixture to make a soft dough. Scoop out about ⅓ of the dough and form a small disc about ½ inch thick. Cut into 8 pie-shaped pieces. Do this for the remaining dough. Place on a cookie sheet lined with parchment paper and bake until done, about 8-12 minutes. Brush with Lime Glaze. Makes about 24 scones.

Scones are served best warm and may be reheated in foil before serving.

Glaze

Melt butter in microwave or on stove. Stir in coconut, brown sugar, lime juice, and rum. Brush glaze over warm scones. Sprinkle with toasted pecans.

Serve with Lime Curd (page 44).

Serve with Lime Curd (page 44).

Ingredients

Scones

- 3 c. self-rising flour
- ½ c. granulated sugar
- 1 stick of unsalted butter
- ½ c. mashed bananas
- ¾ to 1 c. buttermilk

Glaze

- ¼ c. toasted pecans
- ⅛ c. sweetened coconut
- ½ c. packed brown sugar
- 4 t. butter
- 4 t. lime juice
- 4 t. rum or ⅛ t. rum extract

Ingredients

- 2 pkg. frozen spinach
- 1 large onion – finely chopped
- 4-6 cloves of garlic (or to taste) – minced
- ¾ c. butter
- 1 c. flour
- 4 c. chicken stock (we use chicken bouillon to make our stock – provides more intense flavor)
- 7 c. milk
- ½ c. cream
- pepper to taste

Cream of Spinach Soup

Sauté onions and garlic in butter on low heat for about 45 minutes. Stir occasionally so they do not scorch. Add 1 c. flour. Stir in 4 c. chicken stock. Add 6-7 c. of milk and ½ c. cream. Add spinach. Add pepper to taste. Add more milk if soup is too thick. Simmer on low for 1 hour.

This soup is best if made the day before and reheated.

Ingredients

- cucumbers
- filling – either Roasted Garlic and Herb (page 34) or Zesty Caper (page 72)
- lemon pepper – for garnish

Cucumber Striped Flowers

Spread cream cheese filling on bread slices. Strip a cucumber by using a vegetable peeler. Cut into thin strips. Overlap the cucumber strips and place 4-5 strips over the bread. Use a metal cookie cutter and push down hard to cut through cucumber, filling and bread into desired shapes. It works best if you use simple shapes such as stars, flowers, hearts, circles, etc. Sprinkle lemon pepper on top if desired.

Ingredients

- 2 c. cooked chicken, chopped
- ½ c. rosemary
- 3 green onions, chopped
- fresh cracked pepper to taste
- ½ c. parmesan
- 1 c. mayonnaise
- butter
- bread (buttermilk or sourdough)
- parsley for decoration

Rosemary Chicken Tea Sandwiches

Mix together first five ingredients. Add just enough mayonnaise to bind mixture together – about 1 c. Spread butter on bread slices. Add filling and top with second slice. Cut into desired shapes – squares, triangles, etc. Sprinkle parsley or rosemary on sides for decoration.

Ingredients

- 1 3 oz. package cream cheese, softened
- ¼ c. onion, finely chopped
- ¼ c. water chestnuts, finely chopped
- 1 T. mustard
- 2 t. prepared horseradish
- ⅛ t. salt
- dash of pepper
- 6 oz. shaved corned beef, chopped
- 8 slices of pumpernickel bread or rye bread
- butter, softened

Corned Beef Sandwiches

Combine cheese, onion, water chestnuts, mustard, horseradish, salt and pepper. Stir in corned beef. Spread 4 slices of bread with butter. Spread half with corned beef mixture and top with remaining halves. Freeze if desired.

Makes 4 large sandwiches (regular size) or 24 tea sandwiches.

To freeze

Place each large sandwich in a plastic bag. Freeze until ready to use (about 2 weeks maximum). Cut each sandwich into 6 large sandwiches. Thaw before serving.

Pistachio Pudding with Raspberry Jam

Crust

Preheat oven to 350°. Mix together butter, flour, and nuts and press into a 9"x13" pan. Bake for 10-12 minutes. Cool.

Filling

In a large mixing bowl, mix together powdered sugar, cream cheese, pudding mix, milk and rum. Fold in cool whip. Spread filling onto cooled crust.

Freeze and scoop into mini glass cups. Garnish with fresh whipped cream.

Glaze and topping

Combine glaze ingredients and heat in microwave. Drizzle on top of whipped cream. Top with toasted pistachios.

Makes about 40 mini desserts.

This recipe freezes well. Keep in freezer until ready to dish up, then top with whipped cream and garnish.

Ingredients

Crust
- ½ c. butter
- 1 c. flour
- 1 c. walnuts, finely chopped

Filling
- 1 c. powdered sugar
- 8 oz. cream cheese
- 1 c. cool whip
- 2 pkg. (small size) instant pistachio pudding mix
- 2¾ c. milk
- ¼ c. rum (optional)

Glaze
- ¼ jar raspberry seedless jam
- 1 t. orange extract
- ⅓ t. rum
- 1 T. sugar

Topping
- fresh whipped cream
- toasted pistachios

Ingredients

Cake

- 1 box yellow cake mix
- 4 eggs
- ½ c. oil
- 1 (11 oz.) can mandarin oranges, undrained
- ½ c. pecans
- 1 T grated fresh lemon peel
- 3 T. Triple Sec
- 40 small chocolate cups
- Extra mandarin oranges for garnish
- Fresh orange zest

Pineapple Frosting

- 1 small box of instant vanilla pudding
- 1 20 oz. can crushed pineapple, undrained
- 1 8 oz. container of Cool Whip

Mandarin Orange Cake

Preheat oven to 350°. Spray a 9"x13" pan with cooking spray. Combine cake mix, eggs and oil; beat at medium speed with electric mixer until well blended. Add oranges (with juice), triple sec, lemon peel and pecans. Pour batter into pan.

Bake for 20-30 minutes or until done. Cool. Frost with pineapple frosting and refrigerate overnight. Cut into squares and place in chocolate cups if desired. Top with mandarin orange and fresh orange zest.

Pineapple Frosting

Combine pudding mix and pineapple. Beat at medium speed until well blended. Add whipped topping and mix well.

Makes about 40 small tea cakes.

Sea Salt Toffee

Preheat oven to 400°. Line a cookie sheet (with sides) or jelly roll pan with aluminum foil and spray with vegetable spray. Arrange saltines in a single layer on the cookie sheet.

In a saucepan, combine the sugar and butter. Bring to a boil and boil for exactly 3 minutes. Remove from heat and stir in vanilla. Immediately pour caramel mixture over the saltines and spread to cover crackers. Don't worry if it doesn't cover it completely. Sprinkle toffee bits over the caramel. Bake at 400° for 5 minutes. Remove from oven and sprinkle chocolate chips over the top. Let sit for a few minutes and then spread melted chocolate. Top with chopped nuts and sprinkle sea salt. Cool completely and cut/break into pieces.

Save any crumbs (freeze in a plastic bag) to use for ice cream topping.

Ingredients

- 4 oz. saltine crackers (one sleeve)
- 1 c. butter
- 1 c. brown sugar
- 1 t. vanilla
- 1 12 oz. pkg. of toffee bits
- 2 c. semisweet chocolate chips
- ¾ c. chopped pecans, or try walnuts, pecans or almonds
- sea salt

Bourbon Slush

Mix all ingredients together and pour into a container. Place in freezer, stir occasionally until frozen. Take out of freezer about 30 minutes before serving. Serve slush with a spoon.

Ingredients

- 2 c. prepared tea (Assam or Ceylon)
- 1 small can frozen orange juice
- 1 lg. can frozen lemonade
- 1 c. sugar
- 6 c. water
- 2 c. of bourbon

April

Spring Tea Party

❧ Salad

Ginger Carrot Salad

❧ Scones

Strawberry Lemon Scones with Meyer Lemon Glaze

❧ Tea Sandwiches

Pecan Chicken with Grape
Zesty Caper Cucumber
Smoked Cheddar and Ham Apricot Cups

❧ Tea Desserts

Mini Carrot Cream Cheese Tea Cakes
Chocolate Lemon Bars
Lime Spritz Spring Cookies

❧ Tea Suggestions

Sencha Cherry Peach
Lady Day (pomegranate cream)

Ingredients

- 2 c. shredded carrots
- 2 c. shredded beets
- 6 green onions, finely chopped
- 1 T. ginger freshly grated
- 3 T. rice wine
- 1 T. soysauce
- 1 T. sesame oil
- 3 T. toasted sesame seeds

Ginger Carrot Salad

These look darling served in egg cups.

Combine all ingredients together. Make a few hours ahead of time, but tastes best the same day. Strain salad if needed before serving. Place a small scoop in a glass dish or egg cup and sprinkle with sesame seeds.

Makes about 4 c. salad.

Ingredients

- 3 c. self-rising flour
- ½ c. sugar
- 1 stick unsalted butter
- 1 c. buttermilk
- ½ c. sliced strawberries
- 2 T. freshly grated meyer lemon peel or freshly grated regular lemon peel

Glaze

- 1 c. powdered sugar
- 2-3 T. freshly grated meyer lemon peel
- 1-2 T. lemon juice

Strawberry Lemon Scones with Meyer Lemon Glaze

Preheat oven to 400°. Combine self-rising flour and sugar. Cut in butter until mixture is coarse and crumbly. Add strawberries and lemon zest. Add just enough of buttermilk to make a soft dough. Scoop out about ⅓ of the dough and form a small disc about ½ inch thick. Cut into 8 pie-shaped pieces. Do this for the remaining dough. Place on a cookie sheet lined with parchment paper and bake until done, about 8-12 minutes. Makes about 24 scones. Glaze when scones are warm.

Serve with Lemon Curd (page 44) and Devonshire Cream (page 44).

Ingredients

- 2 c. cooked chicken – pulse in food processor or chop finely
- 3 T. green onions, sliced thinly
- ½ c. pecans, chopped
- ½ c. red grapes, sliced in halves
- salt to taste
- mayonnaise
- butter
- bread
- parsley for decoration

Pecan Chicken with Grape Tea Sandwich

Mix together first 5 ingredients. Add just enough mayonnaise to bind the mixture together. Spread butter on bread. Add filling and top with second slice. Cut into desired shapes about 4 tea sandwiches per sandwich. Sprinkle parsley on sides of sandwiches for decoration if desired.

Makes about 16 tea sandwiches.

Ingredients

- ½ c. sour cream
- 8 oz. mayonnaise
- 3 cloves garlic
- ½ t. lemon juice
- 1½ T. capers
- ½ tsp. Tabasco or hot pepper sauce
- 1 T. dried chives

Zesty Caper Cucumber Tea Sandwiches

Combine everything in a food processor except for the sour cream. Blend until thoroughly combined. Fold in sour cream. Process just until mixed. Spread on slices of bread. Chill for several hours or overnight. Trim off crusts. Cut into squares or use a cookie cutter. Garnish witth a slice of cucumber and sprinkle a little lemon pepper over the top.

Smoked Cheddar and Ham Apricot Cups

Beat cream cheese until smooth. Add sour cream. Stir in ham and green onions. Add smoked cheddar. Fill phyllo cups with a dollop of ham salad. Top with a spoonful of preserves Garnish with green onions if desired. Makes 12-15 cups.

- 1 8 oz. pkg. cream cheese softened
- ½ c. sour cream
- 1 c. black forest ham, chopped
- 2 green onions chopped
- ½ c. smoked cheddar cheese, shredded
- 15-20 phyllo cups
- apricot preserves (I like to use Big Spoon Jam Aprium Jam – combination of apricots and plum

Ingredients

Cake

- 1 carrot cake mix
- 1 lg. pkg. instant vanilla pudding
- 4 eggs
- ½ c. cold water
- ½ c. oil
- ¼ t. cloves
- ½ c. brandy
- ¼ c. chopped raisins
- ¼ c. shredded carrots

Glaze

- 4 oz. cream cheese softened
- 1 c. powdered sugar
- water to drizzling consistency

Mini Carrot Cream Cheese Tea Cakes

Preheat oven to 350°. Grease mini bundt pans with flour spray. In a large mixer, combine cake mixes, pudding, eggs, water, oil, cloves, brandy, raisins and carrots. Mix at medium speed for 3 minutes until well blended. Pour into mini bundt pans.

Bake for 9-12 minutes or until done when a toothpick inserted comes out clean. Cool for a few minutes, then invert pan and cool cakes on a wire rack. You may need to run a knife around the edges of the cakes before they will release.

Glaze

Mix together glaze ingredients. Dip cooled cakes into glaze or drizzle glaze over cakes.

Garnish with raisins and shredded carrots. Allow to dry before storing.

Makes about 48 mini tea cakes.

Chocolate Lemon Bars

Preheat oven to 350°.

Spray a 8"x8" pan with cooking spray and then line with foil. Spray foil.

In a bowl or food processor, combine 1 c. flour, ½ c. sugar, butter, lemon peel and salt. Process until mixture forms a ball. If you are doing it by hand, use a fork. Press dough into the prepared pan. Bake about 15-20 minutes or until it starts to lightly brown.

While the crust is baking, combine eggs, sugar, lemon juice, lemon peel, baking powder, and 2 T. flour. Use a whisk for best results. Whisk until well blended. When crust is done, pour filling directly over hot crust and return to oven. Bake about 25-30 minutes or until the center no longer jiggles when you shake it.

Cool bars for about 30 minutes, then refrigerate at least 2 hours before cutting. Dust lemon bars with powdered sugar or drizzle with melted chocolate. Makes 9 large bars or 16 small tea bars. These will freeze well. Cover tightly and freeze up to 1 month.

Ingredients

Crust

- ½ c. butter, softened
- ¼ c. sugar
- 1 c. flour
- 1 T. grated lemon peel, fresh
- ¼ t. salt

Filling

- 2 eggs
- 1 c. sugar
- ¼ c. lemon juice
- 1 T. grated lemon peel, fresh
- ½ t. baking powder
- 2 T. flour

Topping:

- 2 T. powdered sugar
- or ¼ c. chocolate chips, melted in microwave for about 20-40 seconds
- 1-2 t. oil to thin melted chocolate if necessary

Ingredients

Cookies

- 1 c. butter
- ½ c. sugar
- ½ c. brown sugar
- 1 egg
- 2 t. lime peel, grated
- 1 T. lime juice
- 2 t. pure vanilla extract
- ¼ t. baking soda
- ¼ t. salt
- 2½ c. flour
- Jordon almonds or jelly beans for garnish

Lime Glaze

- 1¼ c. powdered sugar
- 1 t. vanilla
- 1 t. lime zest
- 2-4 t. lime juice

Lime Spritz Spring Cookies

These are absolutely refreshing! It's very important to use fresh lime zest for the best flavor.

Cookies

Preheat oven to 400°.

Cream together in a large mixer butter, sugar, and brown sugar. Add egg, lime zest, lime juice, and vanilla. Beat at medium speed in mixer until light and fluffy. Add flour, baking soda and salt. Beat at low speed until soft dough forms.

Scoop with an ice cream scooper (about 1½ inches) into balls. Place on a baking sheet lined with parchment paper about 1 inch apart. Lightly flatten each cookie with the bottom of a glass dipped in sugar.

Bake for about 5 minutes.

Cool completely and frost with lime glaze.

Lime Glaze

Beat glaze ingredients at low speed with electric mixer until smooth. Spread on cookies. Place Jordan Almonds, or jelly beans on top or leave plain and add a bit of zest.

Let dry completely before storing.

Makes about 50 tea cookies.

May

Mother's Day in Mozart

Black Forest Ham Quiche
Asparagus Tarragon Rice Salad

৸ Scones

White Chocolate Raspberry Scones with
Lemon Curd and Devonshire Cream

৸ Tea Sandwiches

Crunchy Almond Chicken Tea Sandwiches
Cucumber Flowers
Strawberry Heart Tea Sandwiches

৸ Tea Desserts

Musical Raspberry Tea Cakes
Crème Brule Tea Buttons
Lemon Blossom Tea Cookies

Tea Suggestions

Almond Fruit Tea Spritzer-iced served in a fluted champagne glass
Duchess Anna
Rhapsody in Raspberry
Moonlight Sonata (cherry/chocolate)

Ingredients

- 2 c. of black forest ham, shredded
- 2 c. Jarlsberg cheese (or any swiss will do), shredded
- 4 eggs
- 1½ c. milk
- 1½ c. whipping cream
- 2 T. flour
- ½ c. red onion, carmelized (page 129)
- 2 T. fresh rosemary chopped to garnish on the top
- 2 9 inch pie shells

Black Forest Ham Quiche

Preheat oven to 350°. Bake shells for about 10 minutes until almost done, but not yet brown. Cool.

In a large mixer, mix together eggs, milk, cream and flour.

For each quiche sprinkle a small handful of cheese over the bottom of half baked crust. This is to prevent the bottom from getting soggy from the onion layer.

Divide and spread about ½ of the caramelized onions between the two crusts. On top of onion layer, add 1 c. ham, then 2 c. of shredded cheese.

Place foil around the pie crusts. (Do not remove during baking). Carefully pour egg mixture over cheese, ham and onion layers. Fill just to top of crust. Sprinkle rosemary on top.

Bake at 350° for about 30 minutes. Then increase heat to 400° and bake for 15-25 more minutes or until completely set (some ovens may take much longer.) If the cheese starts to brown too quickly before the quiche is set, cover entire quiche with tented foil. Quiche is done when it doesn't jiggle anymore. Look carefully or insert a knife to check as cheese may be set, but underneath may not be done.

Enjoy one and freeze the other. To reheat, thaw completely in refrigerator the night before. Cut into 8 pieces before reheating in oven. By cutting the quiche cold, you will be able to get nice exact cuts. Reheat until warm.

Asparagus Tarragon Rice Salad

This recipe was inspired by one of my farmer's market customers.

Wash and cut ends of the asparagus. Slice on the diagonal into about 1 inch pieces. Combine honey and vinegar in a small bowl, set aside.

Place a large skillet over medium heat. Add olive oil. Add pecans and sauté for a few minutes. Add asparagus and cook until barely tender. (You can also cook asparagus in microwave for about 1 minute, then add to pan). Add garlic, green onions and rice. Add honey mixture. Season with salt and pepper. Cook until thoroughly heated. Add tarragon. Serve hot or at room temperature. This is also great with grilled chicken. Make about 10 servings (½ c. each).

- 1½ lb. asparagus
- 4 T. balsamic vinegar
- 3 t. honey
- 2 T. olive oil
- 1 c. pecans, chopped
- 1 garlic clove, minced
- 3 green onions, chopped
- 2 T. tarragon, finely chopped
- 1 t. salt or to taste
- 2 c. brown or wild rice, cooked
- fresh black pepper

Ingredients

- 3 c. self-rising flour
- ½ c. granulated sugar
- 1 stick of unsalted butter
- ¾ to 1 c. buttermilk
- ½ c. raspberries
- ½ c. white chocolate chips
- ½ c. coconut

White Chocolate Raspberry Scones

Preheat oven to 400°. Combine self-rising flour and sugar. Cut in butter until mixture is coarse and crumbly. Mix in raspberries, white chocolate chips, and coconut. Add just enough of buttermilk mixture to make a soft dough. Scoop out about ⅓ of the dough and form a small disc about ½ inch thick. Cut into 8 pie-shaped pieces. Do this for the remaining dough. Or you can cut scones into shapes with simple shaped cookie cutters. Place on a cookie sheet lined with parchment paper and bake until done, about 8-12 minutes . Makes about 24 scones.

Scones are served best warm and may be reheated in foil before serving.

See recipe for Lemon Curd (page 44).

Crunchy Almond Chicken Tea Sandwiches

Mix together first 6 ingredients. Add just enough mayonnaise to bind the mixture together. Spread butter on bread. Add filling and top with second slice. Cut into desired shapes. Sprinkle parsley and slivered almonds on sides of sandwiches for decoration if desired.

Makes about 16 tea sandwiches.

Ingredients

- 2 c. cooked chicken-pulse in food processor, lightly or chop finely
- 3 T. chopped green onions
- ½ c. slivered almonds
- ½ envelope Italian dressing
- ½ t. ginger
- salt and pepper to taste
- mayonaise
- bread
- butter
- parsley for garnish

Cucumber Flowers

Cut cucumbers into flower shapes. Use any of the cucumber fillings and pipe a small rosette onto the cucumber. We used Roasted Garlic and Herb (page 34).

Ingredients

- 3 oz. cream cheese
- 3 green onion, chopped
- 1 t. lemon juice
- 1 garlic clove
- ½ cucumber
- ¼ c. almonds chopped (optional)
- salt and pepper to taste
- ¼ c. sour cream
- strawberries
- butter
- dark rye
- spinach or basil leaves

Strawberry Heart Tea Sandwiches

Place softened cream cheese, green onion, lemon juice, garlic and cucumber into a food processor. Process until smooth. Stir in sour cream and almonds. Butter bread and spread with cream cheese mixture. Trim crusts and cut into 3 long pieces. Cut strawberries into slices (cut it so that it makes a heart shape). Place a strawberry heart shaped slice on top of the cream cheese sandwich and arrange spinach or basil leaf so that it looks like a stem.

Makes about 32 tea sandwiches.

Ingredients

Cupcakes

- 12 oz. of raspberries (frozen or fresh)
- 2 t. sugar
- ¼ c. milk at room temperature
- 4 eggs
- 2 t. vanilla
- 2 c. flour
- 4 T. cornstarch
- 1¾ c. sugar
- 4 t. baking powder
- 1 t. salt
- 1½ sticks of unsalted butter at room temperature

Frosting:

- 2 sticks unsalted butter, room temperature
- 12 ounces cream cheese, room temperature
- 4 c. powdered sugar
- ¾ teaspoon vanilla
- 2 T. reserved raspberry purée

Musical Raspberry Cupcakes

Preheat oven to 350°.

Rinse raspberries and drain completely. Place in a food processor/blender and add 2 t. sugar. Process until smooth. Reserve ¾ c. for the cake.

Line muffin tins with paper liners.

In a small bowl, combine raspberry purée, milk, vanilla. In another small bowl add flour, baking powder, corn starch, salt. Stir to combine.

In a mixing bowl, cream together 1¾ c. sugar and butter. Add eggs. Add about ½ of the flour mixture and blend. Add about ½ of the purée mixture and blend. Blend in the remaining purée and flour mixture. Beat a medium speed for about a minute. Scrape down sides of bowl and beat again for about 30 seconds.

Divide batter evenly among cupcake papers. Bake about 18 minutes or until done. Makes about 24 cupcakes.

Frosting

Beat butter and cream cheese with a mixer on medium-high speed until fluffy, 2 to 3 minutes. Reduce speed to low. Add powdered sugar, 1 cup at a time, and then vanilla. Add in raspberry purée. Mix until smooth.

Accenting the Cupcakes

I went to Michael's Craft Store and bought the Wilton

Continued on page 88

Continued from page 86

Candy Mold Dessert Accents 5 designs #W2102 and a package of Wilton Candy Melts. You can also find them online. Just follow the directions and when hardened add them to the top of your cupcakes.

The cupcake wraps are also from Wilton and can be found at Michael's or online.

Ingredients

Cookies

- 1 c. butter
- 1 c. powdered sugar
- 1 t. salt
- 2 T. Crème Brule loose tea-process in food processor until fine
- 1⅔ c. flour

Frosting

- The Decadent Chocolate Pearl Cake frosting works very well (page 48).

Crème Brule Tea Buttons

Cream butter and powdered sugar together. In a separate bowl mix together flour, salt, loose tea. Add to creamed mixture. Scoop out into cookies (about 1 teaspoon full). Flatten with a glass. Bake at 400° for 5 minutes. Cool completely.

You can also scoop out the cookies and flash freeze on a cookie sheet for about 10 minutes, then transfer to plastic bags and keep on hand until ready to bake. Just thaw for about 10 minutes before baking.

Note: If your cookies tend to spread out too thin while baking, the dough is too warm. You can put the dough in the refrigerator for a bit, or scoop out onto the cookie sheet and freeze for a few minutes before baking. This hardens the butter so they don't spread out as much

To make buttons

Spread a layer of chocolate frosting in between two cookies.

Makes about 40 tea cookies or 20 buttons.

Lemon Blossom Cookies

Preheat oven to 400°. Cream butter, sugar, and brown sugar together. Add egg, lemon peel, lemon juice, and vanilla. Beat at medium speed in mixer until light and fluffy. Add flour, baking soda, and salt. Beat at low speed until soft dough forms. Bake for 5 minutes or until set. Cool completely and frost with lemon glaze. Makes about 60 tea cookies.

Glaze

Combine glaze ingredients and beat at low speed with electric mixer until smooth. Spread or drizzle on cookies. Let dry completely before storing.

Ingredients

- 1 c. butter
- ½ c. granulated sugar
- ½ c. brown sugar
- 1 egg
- 1 t. lemon peel, grated
- 1 T. lemon juice
- 1½ t. pure vanilla extract
- ¼ t. baking soda
- ¼ t. salt
- 2½ c. flour

Glaze:

- 1¼ c. powdered sugar
- 1 t. vanilla
- ½ t. lemon peel
- 2-4 t. lemon juice

Ingredients

- 3 T. loose Assam tea
- 4 cups of boiling water, plus enough cold water to fill a one gallon container
- 1 c. sugar (start with ½ c. cup and add the rest to taste, this is a very sweet tea)
- 1 6 oz. can frozen lemonade
- 2 t. almond extract
- 2 qt. chilled ginger ale

Almond Fruit Tea Spritzer

This is a twist on our almond fruit tea. It makes a nice punch for bridal and baby showers. We served it on Mother's Day and everyone loved it and wanted the recipe. It does have a lot of sugar, so feel free to cut down on the sugar amount if you wish.

Place loose tea in a tea sock or tea infuser. Pour boiling water over the tea leaves. Steep for 4 minutes. Remove leaves from tea. In a one gallon container mix sugar, lemonade and almond extract. Add hot tea. Stir until sugar is dissolved. Fill the container with cold water and/or ice until it reaches half full (2 qts.) Chill. Immediately before serving, add the ginger ale. Serve immediately. This spritzer looks great served in champagne fluted glasses. Add a fresh raspberry for a beautiful effect.

This tea is also good by itself without the ginger ale.

Makes about 1 gallon.

June

June Garden Party Afternoon Tea

❧ Scones

Peach Melba Scones

❧ Tea Sandwiches

Fabulous Bacon Pea Chicken on Croissants
Roasted Asparagus Ham Bundles
Cucumber Flowers

❧ Tea Desserts

Dena's White Chocolate Orange Cupcakes
Coconut Grand Marnier Macaroons
Fruit Pizza Cookie

❧ Tea Suggestions

Southern Hospitalitea (peach, raspberry, vanilla)
Tropical Rainforest Green – Iced

Ingredients

- 3 c. self-rising flour
- ¾ c. granulated sugar
- 1 stick unsalted butter
- ¾ c. buttermilk
- ½ c. fresh peaches sliced
- ½ c. raspberries
- 1 t. vanilla

Glaze

- 1 c. powdered sugar
- 2-3 T. water or milk
- 1 t. vanilla

Peach Melba Scones

Preheat oven to 400°. Mix together flour and sugar. Use pastry cutter to cut in butter. Mixture should resemble coarse cornmeal. Add peaches, raspberries and vanilla. Add just enough buttermilk to make a soft dough. Scoop out about ⅓ of the dough and form a small disc about ½ inch thick. Cut into 8 pie-shaped pieces Do this for the remaining dough. Place on a cookie sheet lined with parchment paper and bake until done, about 8-12 minutes. Makes about 24 scones. Glaze if desired with a mixture of powdered sugar, milk and vanilla. Scones can be stored in a sealed container and reheated in foil.

Recipes for Lemon Curd (page 44) and Devonshire Cream (page 44).

Fabulous Bacon Pea Chicken on Croissants

Mix together first 9 ingredients. Add just enough mayonnaise to bind the mixture together. Spread butter on croissants which have been cut in half or bread. Add filling. If using bread, cut into desired shapes about 4 tea sandwiches per large sandwich. Sprinkle parsley on sides of sandwiches for decoration if desired.

Makes about 16 tea sandwiches.

Note

If you can't find mini croissants, just use a regular size croissant and cut each one in half. Be sure to place a damp paper towel over the croissants before serving. They dry out very quickly..

- 2 c. cooked chicken – pulse in food processor or chop finely
- 3 T. green onions, sliced thinly or use red onion
- ½ - ¾ c. frozen peas
- ½ c. feta
- ½ c. bacon bits
- ¼. c. cashews
- ½ c. celery, chopped
- 1 T. Italian Seasoning
- salt to taste
- mayonnaise
- butter
- mini croissants or slices of bread
- parsley for decoration

Ingredients

- 7 asparagus spears
- 1 sheet puff pastry
- 7 slices of black forest ham
- smoked cheddar cheese, shredded

Roasted Asparagus and Ham Bundles

Preheat oven to 400°.

Thaw puff pastry about 20 minutes. Then cut into 15 strips. (The sheets are folded into thirds. Cut 5 long strips from each third).

Wash asparagus, trim off the ends. Wrap in a wet paper towel and microwave for 30 seconds.

Cut each asparagus spear in half. Lay a piece of ham flat on a cutting board, cut in half. Arrange asparagus on the ham. Sprinkle a bit of smoked cheddar over asparagus. Roll up ham so that the asparagus tip is sticking out. Some will not have tips as they are the end of the asparagus. You can use only the tips if you wish, but you will need more asparagus.

Place each bundle on a cookie sheet lined with parchment paper. Wrap a strip of the puff pastry around each bundle. Or tie up like a bow or knot. Brush pastry with egg. Bake about 10 minutes until puff pastry is done.

Ingredients

- cucumber
- lemon pepper

Cucumber Flowers

Cut cucumbers into flower shapes. Sprinkle with lemon pepper.

Ingredients

Cake

- 1 white cake mix with pudding in the mix
- 1¼ c. water
- ⅓ c. oil
- 3 egg whites
- zest of 1 orange
- 1 t. orange juice
- ¼ c. real mayonnaise
- 1 c. white chocolate chips

Orange Cream Cheese Frosting

- 3 pkg. (8 oz.) cream cheese, softened
- 1 T. orange juice
- 1 t. orange zest
- 4 c. powdered sugar

Dena's Fabulous White Chocolate Orange Cupcakes

These cupcakes are to die for! They are so moist and delicious! Experiment and add your own ingredients.

Cake

Preheat oven to 350°. Combine all cake ingredients in a large mixing bowl. Mix at medium speed for 3 minutes until well blended. Pour into mini cupcake pans lined with mini cupcake papers. Bake for 5-7 minutes or until done when a toothpick inserted comes out clean. Remove from pan and cool before frosting. Makes about 48 mini cupcakes (24 regular cupcake size-bake about 15-18 minutes).

Orange Cream Cheese Frosting

In large bowl beat cream cheese, orange juice, zest until smooth. Gradually add powdered sugar to the mix 1 c. at a time. Continue beating until creamy and smooth in texture. Refrigerate until ready to use. Pipe a rosette onto the top of the cupcakes or frost the cupcake completely and garnish with orange zest..

Coconut Grand Marnier Macaroons

Preheat oven to 350°.

Line cookie sheet with parchment paper. Spray with cooking spray. Mix coconut, vanilla, Grand Marnier and sweetened condensed milk in a large bowl. Drop by spoonfuls onto parchment paper. Bake at 350° for 10 minutes or until set. Cool.

When cool, drizzle melted chocolate chips over top for decoration.

Ingredients

- 1 15 oz. package coconut
- 1 can sweetened condensed milk
- 1 t. vanilla
- 1 T. Grand Marnier (optional)
- 1 c. semisweet chocolate chips, melted

Ingredients

- 2 pkg. refrigerated sugar cookie dough or you can use the Lime Spritz Cookie dough (page 76)
- 1 8 oz. pkg. cream cheese, softened
- ¼ c. powdered sugar
- 1 t. vanilla
- various different kinds of fruit – blueberries, raspberries, grapes, mandarin orange segments, kiwi, etc.

Fruit Pizza

This is a beautiful dessert! When you alternate fruit pieces around the cookie, it looks very professional, even if you aren't an artist!

For a Whole Fruit Pizza

Spray a pizza pan with non-stick spray. Slice cookie dough into thin slices and overlap slices to cover entire pizza pan. Press slices together lightly. Bake at 375° for about 12 minutes or until lightly browned. Cool.

For Individual Fruit Pizzas

Slice cookie dough into thin slices. Line a cookie sheet with parchment paper. Arrange cookies on parchment. Bake according to directions on package. Cool.

In a small bowl, beat together cream cheese, powdered sugar and vanilla until smooth. Spread over cooled cookie dough. Wash and drain fruit very well. Blot fruit with a paper towel. Arrange fruit on top of the cream cheese mixture. It looks best if you start on the outside of the circle and alternate fruit around, then do the next circle inside, each time alternating fruit. Example: blueberry, grape, blueberry all around the outside, then mandarin orange segment, raspberry, mandarin orange segment, etc. then in the middle have a kiwi, etc. If you're doing individual cookies, try to choose small fruit such as blueberries, pomegranate seeds, etc.

Be creative, it really doesn't matter what fruit you use, just alternate each piece and it will turn out beautifully.

When finished, if desired, coat with a glaze of orange marmalade diluted with water. If you do not use fruits which turn brown, such as apples or bananas, you don't need the glaze.

Cut into pizza slices and serve. This does look best when made early in the day and served later. You can make it the day before, but the fruit doesn't look as nice. My advice if you need to prepare it ahead of time: make up the creamed cheese mixture and store in refrigerator, bake the pizza cookie, cool and cover with plastic wrap. Wash fruit and drain it well. On the day of the event, put it all together.

July

Americana Afternoon Tea

∽ Soup

Strawberry Soup

∽ Scones

Blackberry Scones with Lemon Curd and Devonshire Cream

∽ Tea Sandwiches

Apple Walnut Chicken
Watermelon Fruit Compote with Balsamic and Basil
Bacon Cheddar Cream Cheese Cups

∽ Tea Desserts

Summer Heaven Fruit Pie
Chocolate Caramel Bars

∽ Tea Suggestions

English Breakfast
Nilgiri Blue Mountain – Iced
Blue Lady – Iced

Ingredients

- ½ c. orange juice
- 6 oz. vanilla yogurt
- 6 oz. strawberry yogurt
- 3 c. fresh strawberries
- 2 T. honey
- ¼ t. nutmeg, freshly ground is best
- ½ t. cinnamon
- mint leaves and sliced strawberries for garnish

Strawberry Soup

In food processor purée strawberries. Add vanilla and strawberry yogurt, orange juice, honey and spices. Purée until very smooth. Chill. Stand mint leaf up on one side of dish and float a thin slice of strawberry on top. Serve very cold. Enjoy on a hot summer day!

Makes about 3½ c.

Ingredients

- 3 c. self-rising flour
- ½ c. sugar
- 1 stick unsalted butter
- 1 c. buttermilk
- ½ c. blackberries

Glaze

- 1 c. powdered sugar
- 2-3 T. water or fresh lemon juice

Blackberry Scones

Preheat oven to 400°. Mix together self-rising flour and sugar. Cut in butter until mixture is coarse and crumbly. Add blackberries. Add just enough buttermilk to make a soft dough. Scoop out about ⅓ of the dough and form a small disc about ½ inch thick. Cut into 8 pie-shaped pieces. Do this for the remaining dough. Place on a cookie sheet lined with parchment paper and bake until done, about 8-12 minutes. Makes about 24 scones. Brush with glaze while still hot.

Serve with Lemon Curd (page 44) and Devonshire Cream (page 44).

Apple Walnut Chicken Sandwiches

Mix together first five ingredients. Add just enough mayonnaise to bind mixture together. Add salt and pepper to taste. Spread butter on bread. Add filling and top with second slice. Cut into desired shapes – squares, triangles, etc. Butter sides and dip into dried parsley for decoration.

Ingredients

- 2 c. cooked chicken
- 1 apple sliced and chopped
- 1 T. lemon juice
- ¼ c. walnuts
- 3 green onions sliced thinly
- mayonnaise
- butter
- bread
- parsley

Watermelon Fruit Compote with Balsamic and Basil

With a rounded small icecream scoop, scoop out watermelon into small balls. Arrange in a champagne glass. Drizzle balsamic vinegar over watermelon. Garnish with a bit of basil.

Ingredients

- 1 seedless watermelon
- Balsamic vinegar – use a high quality sweet version. I like Coeur D' Olives Black Currant Balsamic Vinegar
- basil leaves for garnish

Ingredients

- 1 8 oz. pkg. cream cheese, softened
- ½ c. sour cream
- 4 slices cooked and crumbled bacon
- ¼ c. grated parmesan cheese
- 2 T. onion, chopped
- 1 T. fresh parsley, chopped
- dark rye bread if making tea sandwiches
- or tomatoes which you use as a tomato cup
- fresh parsley for garnish
- cherry tomatoes cut in half for garnish

Bacon Tomato Cups and/or Sandwiches

There are two different ways to use this filling. You can use it as a filling in a tomato cup or you can use it for tea sandwiches.

Filling

Beat cream cheese until smooth. Gradually add in sour cream. Mix in remaining ingredients. Add salt and pepper to taste. If mixture is still too hard to spread add a bit more sour cream.

Bacon Tomato Cups

To hollow out a tomato, place it upside down on a plate. (That way the tomato stays flat on the plate.) Cut off the very top. Run a knife around the inside edge and scoop out the inside of the tomato. Place a spinach leaf partly inside so that it peeks out over the top. Place a spoonful of filling inside the tomato shell. Sprinkle a few bacon bits on top.

Sandwiches

Butter bread slices. Spread cream cheese mixture on slice. Cut into four slices. Garnish with a cherry tomato half. Makes about 32 tea sandwiches.

Summer Fruit Heaven Pie

Pie

Using an electric mixer, mix the softened cream cheese and sugar until mixed. In another bowl, whip the cream until stiff peaks form. Gently fold the cream into the cream cheese; blend well. Slice the strawberries in half and place on the bottom and sides of a 9 inch deep-dish pie plate. Pour cream cheese mixture over top and chill until firm. Make the blueberry glaze while mixture is chilling.

Blueberry Glaze

Combine blueberries and sugar in a saucepan and cook over low heat until thickened. Be care not to break up the berries too much. Cool to room temperature. Spoon over cheese mixture and and chill several hours or overnight. Or you can cut the pie into small pieces and just spoon the glaze over while warm and serve.

Note: The glaze isn't very thick and dribbles down into the cream cheese mixture.

Pie

- 12 oz. cream cheese softened
- ½ c. sugar
- ½ pint whipping cream
- fresh strawberries

Blueberry Glaze

- 1 pkg. frozen or fresh blueberries 2 c.
- ⅓ c. sugar

Ingredients

- 2 c. unsalted butter
- 3 c. brown sugar
- 2 eggs
- 2½ c. flour
- 1 t. salt
- 1 t. baking soda
- 3 c. oatmeal
- 12 oz. semisweet chocolate chips
- 1 can sweetened condensed milk
- 2 T. butter
- 1 t. vanilla
- 1 c. pecans, chopped

Chocolate Caramel Bars

Line a 9"x13" pan with parchment paper, then spray with cooking spray.

Cream together 1 c. butter, 2 c. brown sugar and eggs. Sift together flour, salt and baking soda. Add to creamed mixture. Stir in oatmeal. Press ¾ of mixture into the 9"x13" pan. (Reserve the remaining ¼ mixture.) Melt together chocolate chips, sweetened condensed milk and 2 T. butter. You can do this on a stove on low heat or in the microwave, 30 seconds at a time, stirring well before microwaving again. Pour chocolate mixture over oatmeal mixture.

In a saucepan combine 1 c. unsalted butter and 1 c. brown sugar. Bring to a boil and boil for 2 minutes stirring constantly. The mixture will get bubbly and foamy. Turn off heat and add vanilla. Immediately pour over chocolate layer. Sprinkle chopped pecans over caramel layer. Crumble/chunk the reserved oatmeal mixture on the top of the caramel/chocolate mixture. Bake at 350° for 20 minutes. Do not over-bake. The top oatmeal chunky layer will be almost done.

Let set overnight or refrigerate for a few hours. Take a knife and run along the edges. Flip pan over to release bars. Peel off paper and flip over so that bars are right side up. Cut into 40 bars.

For best results, let set overnight before cutting, otherwise they will be too gooey.

August

August Afternoon Tea

✑ Scones

Coconut Mango Scones

✑ Tea Sandwiches

Cilantro Black Bean Salad in Corn Shells
Shrimp Cucumber Salsa in an Avocado Boats
Jalapeño Bacon Mini Muffins with Sourcream Topping

✑ Tea Desserts

Margarita Pie
Pecan Sandies

✑ Tea Suggestions

Strawberry Mango Margarita Tea
Island Nights
Wuyi Mountain Oolong Blend

Ingredients

- 3 c. self-rising flour
- ½ c. granulated sugar
- 1 stick unsalted butter
- ½ c. buttermilk
- 2 c. mangos, chopped
- 1 c. coconut
- ½ c. plus 2 T. mango juice
- 1 c. powdered sugar

Coconut Mango Scones

Preheat oven to 400°. Mix together self-rising flour and sugar. Cut in butter until mixture is coarse and crumbly. Add mangos and coconut. Add ½ c. of the mango juice and just enough buttermilk (about ½ c.) to make a soft dough. Scoop out about ⅓ of the dough and form a small disc about ½ inch thick. Cut into 8 pie-shaped pieces. Do this for the remaining dough. Place on a cookie sheet lined with parchment paper and bake until done, about 8-12 minutes. Makes about 24 scones. Brush with glaze while still hot. Scones can be stored in a sealed container and reheated in foil.

Serve with Lemon Curd (page 44) and Devonshire Cream (page 44).

Glaze

Mix 1 c. powdered sugar and 2 T. mango juice. Drizzle over warm scones.

Cilantro Black Bean Salad in a Corn Shell

Preheat oven to 400°. Spray baking pan with cooking spray. Arrange seeds on baking pan. Spray seeds with Pam. Sprinkle cumin, garlic salt and seasoning salt over seeds. Bake for 3-5 minutes or until toasted.

Dressing

Combine in a large bowl all of the dressing ingredients, except the water. Use an immersion blender or food processor and process until smooth. Add enough water to desired consistency.

Salad

Mix beans, corn, olives, green onion, tomato and cheddar cheese in a large bowl. Add spinach, dressing to taste and toss. Enjoy!

Shells

Preheat oven to 400°.

Spray muffin tins with cooking spray. Place tortilla or taquito shells in each muffin tin. Try to roll them into a cone shape. They may break slightly when you put them in, that's okay. Bake for 10-15 minutes. Cool. Fill shells with salad and top with pumpkin seeds. Drizzle a little dressing over the top.

Ingredients

- 1 can black beans
- 1 can corn
- 1 small can black olives, sliced
- ½ c. green onions, chopped
- 2 small Roma tomatoes
- 1 c. cheddar cheese – cut into small cubes
- 1 small bag fresh spinach finely chopped
- 1 cup pumpkin seeds
- cumin
- garlic salt
- seasoning salt

Dressing

- 1 t. garlic powder
- 2 garlic cloves, peeled
- ½ t. black pepper
- 1 t. aeasoning salt
- 1½ c. vegetable oil
- ⅓ c. red wine vinegar
- ½ c. parmesan cheese
- 3 small bunches cilantro, chopped
- ½ c. mayonnaise
- ¼ c. water – more or less to thin dressing to desired consistency

Shells

- 4 inch or smaller tortilla shells or taquitos

Ingredients

- 36 small shrimp, cooked (can be frozen)
- ½ c. red onion
- 2 medium tomatoes, finely chopped
- ½ c. cilantro, finely chopped
- ½ small jalapeño (more or less depending upon taste)
- 1 clove garlic, finely chopped
- ½ cucumber finely chopped
- juice of one lime
- 4 avocados – the smallest ones you can find

Cucumber Shrimp Salsa in an Avocado Boat

In a medium bowl, combine all ingredients except avocados. Immediately before serving, cut each avocado in half. Carefully scoop out the avocado and chop into small pieces, add to salsa. Spoon salsa into each avocado half. Serve immediately. Makes about 8 small boats.

Jalapeño Bacon Mini Muffin with Sour Cream Topping

Preheat oven to 375°.

Mix together first 12 ingredients and pour into greased mini muffins tins, greased 9"x13" pan or combination. I like to make about 24 mini muffins and pour the rest into a 9"x13" pan (I freeze the extra).

Bake for about 8-10 min for the mini muffins or 45 min for the 9"x13". Cool mini muffins for a few minutes in pan before removing them. To make topping, combine sour cream and taco seasoning (or use a bit of cumin). When muffins are cool, top with sour cream mixture. Sprinkle a little cumin over the top for garnish.

Ingredients

- 3 (7 oz.) packages of cornbread mix
- 1 red onion, finely chopped
- 2 c. shredded sharp cheddar cheese
- 2 eggs, beaten
- 2½ c. buttermilk
- ½ c. vegetable oil
- 1 15 oz. creamed corn
- 6 oz. jalapeño, chopped
- 3 T. bacon
- ½ c. green chilies
- ⅓ t. salt
- pepper

Topping

- ½ c. sour cream
- 1 T. taco seasoning

Ingredients

- ½ c. butter
- 1¼ c. crushed pretzels
- ¼ c. sugar
- 1 (14 oz.) can sweetened condensed milk
- 2 T. lime juice
- 1 T. lemon juice
- 3 T. tequila
- 3 T. triple sec
- 1 c. whipping cream – whipped in a separate bowl until very stiff
- additional whipping cream for garnish
- slices of fresh lime

Margarita Pie

In small bowl melt butter in the microwave. Stir in pretzel crumbs and sugar. Mix well. Press crumbs on bottom of 9"x9" pan. Chill.

In large bowl, combine sweetened condensed milk, lime juice, lemon juice, tequila, and triple sec; mix well. Fold in whipped cream. Pour into crust. Freeze until firm overnight in freezer. Thaw slightly before cutting. Cut into squares and place in small glass dishes. Garnish with additional whipped cream and a slice of lime.

Makes 16-20 tea desserts.

Ingredients

- 2 c. butter
- 1 c. powdered sugar
- 1 c. brown sugar
- 1½ t. salt
- 2 c. finely chopped pecans
- 3⅓ c. flour

Pecan Sandies

Preheat oven to 350°.

Cream together in a large mixer butter, powdered sugar and brown sugar. In a small bowl, combine, salt, and flour. Add flour mixture to creamed mixture. Stir in pecans. Scoop with an ice cream scooper into balls(about 1 inch in diameter). Place on a baking sheet lined with parchment paper about 1 inch apart. Bake for 6-7 minutes or until done. Sprinkle with powdered sugar if desired. Makes about 84 cookies.

September

September Savory Tea

ෆ Soup

Roasted Carrot Soup

ෆ Quiche

Black Forest Ham Quiche

ෆ Scones

Cinnamon Apple Pecan Scones

ෆ Tea Suggestions

Apple Autumn Spice
Crème Brule Chocolate Chai

Ingredients

- 4 t. butter, melted
- ½ t. black pepper
- 2 pounds carrots cut into 2 inch pieces
- 1½ c. water
- 2 t. chopped oregano or ½ t. dried oregano
- 1 t. butter
- ½ t. cumin
- 1½ T. honey
- 1 T. fresh lime juice
- 2 (14½ oz.) can vegetable/chicken broth

Roasted Carrot Soup

Preheat oven to 400°. Combine 4 t. melted butter, pepper and carrots in a shallow roasting pan coated with cooking spray; toss to coat. Bake at 400° for 35 minutes or until tender, stirring every 10 minutes.

Place carrot mixture, water and oregano in a food processor, process until smooth.

Melt 1 t. butter in a large saucepan over medium heat. Add the cumin, cook 30 seconds or until fragrant, stirring constantly. Add puréed carrot mixture, honey, lime juice, and broth. Bring to a simmer over medium heat.

Makes about 10-12 servings.

Black Forest Ham Quiche

See recipe on page 80.

Cinnamon Apple Scones

Preheat oven to 400°. Mix together self-rising flour and sugar. Cut in butter until mixture is coarse and crumbly. Add apples and cinnamon. Add just enough buttermilk to make a soft dough. Scoop out about ⅓ of the dough and form a small disc about ½ inch thick. Cut into 8 pie-shaped pieces. Do this for the remaining dough. Place on a cookie sheet lined with parchment paper. Add a spoonful of topping to each scone. Press down lightly and bake until done, about 8-12 minutes or longer depending on your oven. Makes about 24 scones.

Topping

Mix together topping ingredients, place 1-2 T. of topping on each scone.

Serve with Lemon Curd (page 44) and Devonshire Cream (page 44).

Ingredients

- 3 c. self-rising flour
- ½ c. sugar
- 1 c. chopped apples
- 1 t. cinnamon
- 1 stick unsalted butter
- 1 c. buttermilk (sometimes you may need to add a bit more)

Topping

- ¼ c. butter, softened
- ½ c. brown sugar
- 2 T. flour
- ¼ c. oatmeal
- 1 t. cinnamon
- pecans (optional)

October

Harvest Afternoon Tea

❧ Soup

Sweet Potato Soup Served in Pumpkin Bowls

❧ Scones

Pumpkin Pecan Scones

❧ Tea Sandwiches

Sesame Chicken
Blue Cheese Mushroom Pillows
Olive Pecan Savory

❧ Tea Desserts

Blackberry Cobbler Pie
Chocolate Snaps
Spice Cake Cookies

❧ Tea Suggestions

Pumpkin Crème or Pumpkin Masala Chai
Orange Cranberry Spice
Harmutty Assam

Ingredients

- 2-3 cloves of garlic
- ½ onion, chopped
- ¼ c. butter
- ¼ c. flour
- 3 c. chicken broth
- 2 c. milk
- ½ c. whipping cream
- 5-8 sweet potatoes or yams (depending on size)
- ¼ c. green onions – finely chopped for garnish
- 1-2 t. curry

Sweet Potato Soup

Wash sweet potatoes. Cut off the ends and poke holes in each with a knife. Microwave for 20 minutes or until soft.

Sauté garlic, onion and butter until golden about 25 minutes. Add flour. Cook another 2 minutes. Add chicken broth, milk and cream and stir until smooth. Peel sweet potatoes and add to broth mixture. Purée mixture with an immersion blender or food processor. Add 1-2 t. curry depending on your taste. Heat mixture until warmed, but do not boil as it will curdle. Garnish with the green onion. Enjoy! I love to serve this soup in tiny carved out pumpkins.

Ingredients

- 3 c. self-rising flour
- ½ c. sugar
- 2 T. cinnamon
- ¾ c. of toasted pecan pieces
- 1 stick unsalted butter
- 1 c. canned pumpkin
- ¾ c. buttermilk

Glaze

- 1 c. powdered sugar
- 2-3 T. water or milk

Pumpkin Pecan Scones

Preheat oven to 400°. Mix together self-rising flour and sugar. Cut in butter until mixture is coarse and crumbly. Add cinnamon, pumpkin and pecans. Add just enough buttermilk to make a soft dough. Scoop out about ⅓ of the dough and form a small disc about ½ inch thick. Cut into 8 pie-shaped pieces. Do this for the remaining dough. Place on a cookie sheet lined with parchment paper and bake until done, about 8-12 minutes. Makes about 24 scones. Brush with glaze while still hot.

Serve with Lemon Curd (page 44) and Devonshire Cream (page 44).

Sesame Chicken Sandwiches

Mix together first four ingredients. Add just enough mayonnaise to bind mixture together. Spread butter on bread. Add filling and top with second slice. Cut into desired shapes-squares, triangles, etc. about 4 tea sandwiches per sandwich. Butter sides and sprinkle sesame seeds on edges for decoration.

Makes about 16 tea sandwiches.

Ingredients

- 2 c. cooked chicken
- 2 T. sesame seed oil
- 3 T. green onions, sliced thinly
- ¼ c. chopped cilantro
- mayonnaise
- sesame seeds
- butter
- 8 slices of bread

Blue Cheese Mushroom Pillows

Thaw pastry sheets about 30 minutes.

While pastry is thawing, sauté onions in butter for about 20-30 minutes until the onions start to caramelize. Start with medium high heat, then reduce to low. Continue to stir until onions become brown and carmelized. Add mushrooms and sauté until done.

Cut puff pastry into 3 equal long rectangles (follow the folding guide). Cut each rectangle into 3 square pieces. Place on a cookie sheet lined with parchment paper. Add a small spoonful of mushrooms and onions, top with a bit of blue cheese. Fold over and seal with fingers or fork. At this point you can freeze them if you wish. If you plan on freezing them, flash freeze them first by putting the cookie sheet into the freezer and freezing directly for at least 15

Ingredients

- 1 package puff pastry
- ½ red onion, chopped
- 2 T. butter
- 9 T. blue cheese, crumbled
- 4 mushrooms, finely chopped

Continued on page 130

Continued from page 129

minutes. Then transfer each pastry to ziplock freezer bags and keep in freezer until ready to use.

When ready to bake, place on a cookie sheet lined with parchment paper. Thaw for about 15 minutes. Brush with beaten egg.

Bake at 400° until golden (about 10-20 min depending on size). Makes 9 triangles.

Ingredients

- 1 8 oz. pkg. cream cheese softened
- ½ c. sour cream
- ½ c. chopped pecans
- 1 c. chopped green olives
- ¼ t. pepper
- rye/sourdough/dark or white bread

Olive Pecan Savory

Beat cream cheese until smooth. Add sour cream. Stir in pecans, green olives, pepper. Butter bread. Spread on cream cheese mixture. Garnish with a slice of olive. This works well as an open faced sandwich, but for a different look, you could use 2 slices of bread and have a closed sandwich. The dark rye bread makes a nice contrast with the white spread.

Blackberry Cobbler Pie

Preheat oven to 375°.

In a food processor add butter Crisco, salt, and flour. Pulse. Slowly add warm water a little at a time. Pulse until mixture is combined. Divide into 2 balls. Roll one ball into a piecrust (or if you are scooping out the dessert into small glass dishes, you can just press the dough into the pie plate).

Combine sugar, flour and salt. Add sugar mixture to blackberries and mix well. Fill pie crust with mixture.

Roll out second ball of pie crust. Cut into strips or if serving in glass dishes just cut into squares. Place strips or squares over filling. Bake for 35 minutes or until crust is golden brown.

Cool on a wire rack. Scoop into dessert dishes and top with whipped cream. Garnish with a blackberry and a bit of fresh lemon zest.

Ingredients

- 1¼ c. sugar
- ¼ c. flour
- ¼ t. salt
- 4 c. blackberries, fresh or frozen
- 1 t. vanilla

Crust

- 1½ sticks butter Crisco
- 2 t. salt
- 3 c. flour
- ½ c. water, warm
- fresh lemon zest

Ingredients

- 1 pkg. of Devil's Food Cake Mix
- ⅓ c. oil
- 2 eggs, lightly beaten
- 1 t. ground ginger
- 1-3 t. pepper
- 1 t. cinnamon
- 1 T. water
- ¾ c. chocolate chips
- ¼ c. sugar

Chocolate Snaps

Preheat oven to 375°. Combine first 7 ingredients in a large bowl.

Mix until smooth. Stir in chocolate chips. Use a 1½ inch ice cream scoop and scoop into balls. Spray scoop with cooking spray first. Roll balls in granulated sugar to coat. Place balls 2 inches apart on a lightly greased baking sheet. Bake for 8-10 minutes. Cool 2-3 minutes on baking sheets before removing. You can also freeze the balls before baking. Just thaw for 10-15 minutes and roll in sugar then bake as usual. If you like a flatter cookie, use a glass dipped in sugar and flatten before baking.

Makes about 4 dozen cookies.

Ingredients

Cookies

- 1 box (18.25 oz.) spice cake mix
- 2 eggs
- ½ c. unsalted butter, melted
- 2 T. flour
- 1 c. white chocolate chips
- ½ c. chopped pecans

Glaze

- 1-2 t. oil
- 1 c. white chocolate chips melted

Spice Cake Cookies

Cookies

Preheat oven to 350°. Line baking sheets with parchment paper. In a large bowl, combine cake mix, eggs, melted butter and flour. Stir in chocolate chips and nuts. Drop dough by rounded tablespoons or use a 1½ inch small ice cream scoop. Bake for 7-10 minutes or until done. Makes about 7 dozen cookies.

Glaze

Melt white chocolate chips in the microwave at ½ power for 20 seconds. Stir well beating with a spoon. Put back into microwave and microwave 20 seconds more. If still not melted, do again until all the chips are melted. Use a teaspoon of oil to thin chocolate to desired consistency if needed. Stir again. Drizzle cooled cookies with melted white chocolate.

November

Be Thankful for Your Friends Afternoon Tea

Black Forest Ham Quiche
Tomato Basil Bisque

↬ Scones

Cranberry Orange Scones or
Pumpkin Pecan Scones

↬ Tea Sandwiches

Smoked Turkey with Homemade Cranberry Mustard
Artichoke Savory

↬ Tea Desserts

White Chocolate Cranberry Bars
Cappuccino Brownies
Pumpkin Pie Cake

↬ Tea Suggestions

Pumpkin Crème
Hazelnut Vanilla
Heaven's Treasure Golden Yunnan

Tomato Basil Bisque

Please see recipe on page 42.

Black Forest Ham Quiche

Please see recipe on page 80.

Cranberry Orange Scones

Ingredients

- 3 c. self-rising flour
- ½ c. sugar
- 1 stick unsalted butter
- ¾ c. - 1 c. buttermilk
- ¼ c. orange juice
- ½ c. chopped cranberries (use fresh, freeze until firm and then chop in food processor)
- zest of 1 orange

Glaze

- 1 c. powdered sugar
- 2-3 T. orange juice

Preheat oven to 400°. Combine self-rising flour and sugar. Cut in butter until mixture is coarse and crumbly. Add cranberries and orange zest or peel. Add orange juice to ½ c. buttermilk. Stir this mixture into the flour mixture to make a soft dough. If mixture is too dry, add more buttermilk. Scoop out about ⅓ of the dough and form a small disc about ½ inch thick. Cut into 8 pie-shaped pieces. Do this for the remaining dough. Place on a cookie sheet lined with parchment paper and bake until done, about 8-12 minutes. Makes about 24 scones. Brush with glaze while still hot.

Serve with Lemon Curd (page 44) and Devonshire Cream (page 44).

Pumpkin Pecan Scones

Please see recipe on page 128.

Smoked Turkey with Homemade Cranberry Mustard

Mustard

Soak the seeds in the water and vinegar for at least 12 hours. In a saucepan combine cranberries, syrup, salt, allspice and cloves. Bring mixture to a quick boil until cranberries pop open, turn on low for a few more minutes. Cool.

In a food processor combine, cranberry mixture and mustard seeds. Thoroughly blend together for about 2 minutes or until mustard seeds are coarsely ground. Transfer to sterile container and store up to 2 months in the refrigerator. Don't worry if the mustard is too spicy, it willl mellow after a few days.

Sandwiches

Spread a thin amount of cranberry mustard on both sides of the bread. Top one slice with turkey/chicken, cheese, spinach leaves. Trim crusts and cut each sandwich into 4 pieces. Use a toothpick to secure sandwiches.

Ingredients

Mustard

- ½ c. yellow mustard seeds
- ½ c. white wine vinegar
- ¼ c. water
- ¼-½ c. cranberries
- ¼ c. maple syrup
- 1 t. salt
- 1 t. allspice
- 1 t. cloves

Sandwich

- sliced turkey or chicken breast
- smoked cheddar cheese
- spinach leaves
- dark rye /sour dough/ or do a mixture of both for a unique effect

Ingredients

- 1 8 oz. pkg. cream cheese, softened
- ½ c. sour cream
- ½ c. mayonnaise
- 1 small jar marinated artichokes, well-drained, chopped
- 5 cloves garlic, minced
- 1 c. parmesan, grated
- salt and pepper to taste
- butter
- bread slices (sour dough tastes great with this filling)
- artichoke pieces and grated parmesan for garnish

Artichoke Savory Tea Sandwiches

Beat cream cheese in a large mixer until smooth. Gradually add in sour cream and mayonnaise. Mix in artichokes, garlic, and parmesan. Add salt and pepper to taste. Spread butter on bread. Spread filling on buttered slice.Cut into four slices. Garnish with a piece of artichoke or parmesan cheese.

This recipe makes about 40 tea sandwiches if you cut each large sandwich slice into 4.

White Chocolate Cranberry Bars

Combine crushed graham crackers and melted butter. Press mixture into the bottom of a 9"x13" pan. Pour one can of sweetened condensed milk over crumb mixture. Layer with 1 c. coconut, 1 c. dried cranberries, ½ c. walnuts, and 1 c. white chocolate chips. Press mixture down with hands. Pour one can of sweetened condensed milk over the top of the ingredients. Repeat process: 1 c. coconut, 1 c. dried cranberries, ½ c. walnuts, and 1 c. white chocolate chips. Press mixture down again with hands. Top with the combination of white chocolate chips and dried cranberries. Press down again with hands. Bake at 350° for about 18 minutes and browned lightly. Cool and then refrigerate until firm, preferably overnight. Cut into bars. Makes about 24-36 depending on the cut size.

Ingredients

Bars

- 4 c. crushed graham crackers
- ½ c. melted butter
- 2 c. shredded coconut
- 2 c. dried cranberries
- 1 c. walnuts, chopped
- 2 c. white chocolate chips
- 2 cans sweetened condensed milk

Topping

- ½ c. mixture of white chocolate chips and chopped dried cranberries.

Cappuccino Brownies

Brownies

Follow directions according to package and add instant coffee mixture or brewed coffee. Cool completely. Cut into squares. Pipe a small rosette on each brownie with Cappuccino Frosting. For garnish add a chocolate chip (white or brown) in the center of each rosette.

Cappuccino Frosting

Cream butter and powdered sugar together with a mixer. Add vanilla and coffee, mix well. If frosting seems too thick, thin with a bit more coffee.

Ingredients

Brownie

- 1 pkg. brownie mix
- 1 T. instant coffee or more to taste dissolved in 1 T. water ot 1 T. brewed coffee

Cappuccino Frosting

- 1 1b. box of powdered sugar
- ½ c. butter-softened
- 1 t. vanilla
- 1 T. instant coffee dissolved in 1-2 T. water or 1T. brewed coffee
- chocolate chips for decoration (white or dark)

Ingredients

- 3 eggs
- 1 15 oz. can pumpkin
- 1 12 oz.can evaporated milk
- 1 c. sugar
- ⅛ t. salt
- 1½ t. cinnamon
- 1 t. ginger
- 1 T. vanilla extract
- 1box yellow cake mix
- 1¼ c. butter, melted
- 1 c. chopped nuts, pecans are wonderful

Pumpkin Pie Cake

My kids adore this dessert warm, but I actually think it tastes better after it's been in the refrigerator for a few hours. Preheat oven to 350°. Mix together first 8 ingredients. Pour into a 9"x13" ungreased baking dish. Sprinkle cake mix on top. Do not stir. (Yes, really!) Drizzle with melted butter. Bake at 350° for 25 minutes. Top with nuts and bake another 15 minutes or until firm.

Serve hot or cold. Scoop into dishes and top with whipped cream. Garnish with a bit of cinnamon.

December

Holiday Afternoon Tea

Black Forest Ham Quiche

✍ Scones

White Chocolate Raspberry Scones or
Cranberry Orange Scones

✍ Tea Sandwiches

Smoked Almond Cranberry Chicken
Striped Christmas Cucumber Trees
Layered Spinach Bow Sandwiches

✍ Tea Desserts

Eggnog Tea Cakes
Shimmering Golden Rum Balls
Peppermint Brittle
Cranberry Orange Bliss Cookies

✍ Tea Suggestions

Candy Cane Chai
Ceylon
Christmas Spice

Black Forest Ham Quiche

Please see recipe on page 80.

White Chocolate Raspberry Scones

Please see recipe on page 82.

Cranberry Orange Scones

Please see recipe on page 138.

Smoked Almond Cranberry Chicken Tea Sandwiches

Mix together first five ingredients. Add just enough mayonnaise to bind mixture together-about 1 c. Spread butter on bread slices. Add filling and top with second slice. Cut into desired shapes-squares, triangles, etc. Butter sides and dip into finely chopped almonds.

Ingredients

- 3 c. cooked chicken – chopped
- 3 green onions chopped (use white and green parts)
- ¾ c. sharp white cheddar cheese – shredded
- ½ c. smoked almonds chopped finely
- ¾ c. dried sweetened cranberries
- 1 c. mayonnaise
- pepper
- butter
- bread (potato, buttermilk, sourdough)
- finely chopped smoked almonds for decoration

Striped Cucumber Trees

Spread filling on bread slices. Strip a cucumber by using a vegetable peeler. Cut into thin strips. Overlap cucumber strips and place 4-5 cucumber strips over the bread. Use a cookie cutter or knife to cut into tree shape. Cut a piece of small tomato or red pepper into "garland". Arrange on top of cucumber.

Ingredients

- cucumber filling (Roasted Garlic and Herb (page 34) recipe or Zesty Caper (page 72))
- cream cheese, softened
- cucumber
- bread

149

Ingredients

- 1 pkg. frozen chopped spinach, thawed and squeezed dry
- 1 pkg. dry vegetable soup mix
- 1 small carton sour cream
- 1 small can water chestnuts, chopped
- 1 small jar pimento
- 8 oz. sharp cheddar cheese, grated
- 1 c. mayonnaise
- 3 oz. cream cheese, softened
- pepper to taste
- white and dark rye bread slices
- 1 cucumber for garnish
- 1 tomato or red pepper for garnish

Layered Spinach Bow Sandwiches

Make spinach filling by combining dry soup mix with sour cream and mayonnaise. Add thawed spinach. Be sure to remove the excess water by blotting with paper towels, otherwise your filling will be too watery. Add chopped water chestnuts. Drain pimento well and add remaining ingredients.

To assemble sandwiches, spread a white slice of bread with the spinach mixture. Top with a dark slice, then spread with another layer of the spinach mixture. Top again with another slice of white. These are very pretty 3 layer ribbon sandwiches.

Note

Make sure that the white slices are on the outside and the dark slice is in the middle, otherwise you won't see the slice in the middle because the filling is mostly white. These sandwiches cut best when refrigerated overnight. Place large sandwiches on a cookie sheet, top with a piece of parchment, then with a damp paper towel. Wrap in plastic wrap and chill overnight. The next day, cut each sandwich into 4 squares. Peel a cucumber into a long strip. Cut a very thin "string" from the peel. Form into a bow. Use a little cream cheese or mayonnaise to "stick" the bow to the sandwich. Place a piece of tomato or pepper in the middle of the bow. Use cream cheese or mayonnaise for "glue" again if needed.

Eggnog Tea Cakes

Preheat oven to 350°. Spray mini bundt pans with flour baking spray.

In a large mixing bowl, combine cake mix, eggnog, oil, eggs, rum, nutmeg and mayonnaise. Beat at medium speed for about 4 minutes. Pour into mini bundt pans (12 to a pan). Bake about 8-10 minutes until done (when an inserted toothpick comes out clean). Cool.

Mix together glaze ingredients except nutmeg. Use more eggnog if you need to dilute glaze. Dip cakes into glaze and allow to set. Sprinkle with nutmeg.

Makes about 45 mini cakes.

Cake

- 1 pkg. yellow cake mix
- 1 c. eggnog
- ¼ c.vegetable oil
- 3 eggs
- 2 T. spiced rum
- ½ t. nutmeg
- 2 T. mayonnaise

Glaze

- 3 c. powdered sugar
- ½ c. eggnog
- 2 T. rum
- ¼ t. nutmeg

Ingredients

- 3 c. toasted pecans, walnuts, hazelnuts
- 2½ c. finely crushed vanilla wafers (use food processor to chop)
- 1 c. powdered sugar
- 4 T. cocoa powder
- 4 T. light corn syrup
- ½ c. spiced rum

Coating

- 1 c. powdered sugar saved for later use or use gold sugar

Shimmering Golden Rum Balls

Preheat oven to 350°. Place nuts on a cookie sheet and toast 5-8 minutes until lightly browned, do not over bake. Cool completely then chop finely.

Combine all ingredients together, mixing well. Chill for about 1 hour. Shape into 1 inch balls using a melon baller or small ice cream scoop. Roll balls in ½ c. powdered sugar or gold sugar. Store in an airtight container in the refrigerator. Serve at room temperature.

These taste better if made a few days ahead of time. They will keep about 2 weeks. You can reroll them in more powdered sugar if needed. Makes about 8 dozen balls.

Peppermint Brittle

Preheat oven to 350°. Line a baking sheet with parchment paper. Spray parchment and corners with cooking spray.

In a medium mixing bowl, stir together flour, baking soda and salt. In a large bowl stir in melted butter, both sugars and vanilla until smooth. Stir in flour mixture until just blended. Stir in 2 c. white chocolate chips and 1 c. crushed candy canes. Press dough onto parchment paper on cookie sheet.

Bake for about 15-20 minutes until dough looks just barely set and golden. Be careful not to bake too long otherwise they will be hard to cut.

Before brittle is totally cool, take a knife and score the brittle into pieces. Allow to finish cooling. When cool, melt 1 c. white chocolate chips in microwave 30 sec at a time until melted. Drizzle over brittle. If you need to thin the chocolate glaze, add a few drops of vegetable oil to chocolate. Sprinkle remaining peppermint pieces over glaze and allow to set. This recipe makes about 55 pieces. I like to cut mine in squares and then diagonally into triangle pieces.

- 3 cups flour
- 1 cup sugar
- 1 t. baking soda
- ⅔ cup brown sugar
- ½ t. salt
- 2 t. vanilla
- 3 cups white chocolate chips
- 1-3 t. vegetable oil (to thin topping)
- 2 cups. small candy canes crushed (put them in a ziplock bag and crush them with a hammer)
- 1½ cup unsalted butter – melted and cooled slightly

Ingredients

- 2 c. butter, softened
- 1 c. sugar
- 1 c. brown sugar
- 2 eggs
- 2 t. orange peel, grated
- 2 T. orange juice (or cranberry juice)
- 3 t. pure vanilla extract
- ½ t. baking soda
- ½ t. salt
- 5 c. flour
- 1 c. cranberries, dried
- 1 c. white chocolate chips

Glaze

- 1¼ c. powdered sugar
- 1-2 t. pure vanilla extract
- 1 t. orange peel, grated
- 2-4 t. orange juice

Cranberry Orange Bliss Cookies

Preheat oven to 375°. Cream butter, sugar and brown sugar together. Add eggs, orange peel, orange juice and vanilla. Beat at medium speed in mixer until light and fluffy. Add flour, baking soda and salt. Beat at low speed until soft dough forms.Scoop into balls and place on a cookie sheet lined with parchment paper. Bake for 5-6 minutes. Cool completely and frost with orange glaze.

Glaze

Mix powdered sugar, vanilla, orange peel and orange juice to desired consistency. Beat at low speed with an electric mixer until smooth. Drizzle on cookies. Let dry completely before storing.

Index

About the Author

Amy Lawrence is an example for women who have had many successful careers in life, including teacher and business owner. With a master's degree in Special Education, she taught for 11 years. In 2003 Amy decided to pursue her passion and opened her tea room, An Afternoon to Remember. Her tea room won many awards including Best Small Tea Room in the U.S. in 2006, KCRA's A-List in 2007, 2008 and 2009, and Sacramento Magazine's Best Tea Room in 2008.

Amy owned and operated her tea room for almost 7 years before transitioning full time to her on-line and wholesale tea company, Afternoon to Remember Fine Teas and Gifts. Her company carries over 150 fine loose leaf teas, many of Amy's own blends. In addition to running her tea company she writes cookbooks, resource books for tea room owners as well as teaches classes. She has published eleven books and has sold more than 15,000 of them. Amy currently lives in the Seattle area where you can find her selling fine teas at her tea shop in Bothell as well as online at www.afternoontoremember.com.

Also from ATR Publishing

Creating an Afternoon
to Remember

A Little of This and a
Little of That

Making it Your Own
Afternoon to Remember

Tea Time Tidbits
and Treats

Drop by for Tea

Master Tea Room
Recipes